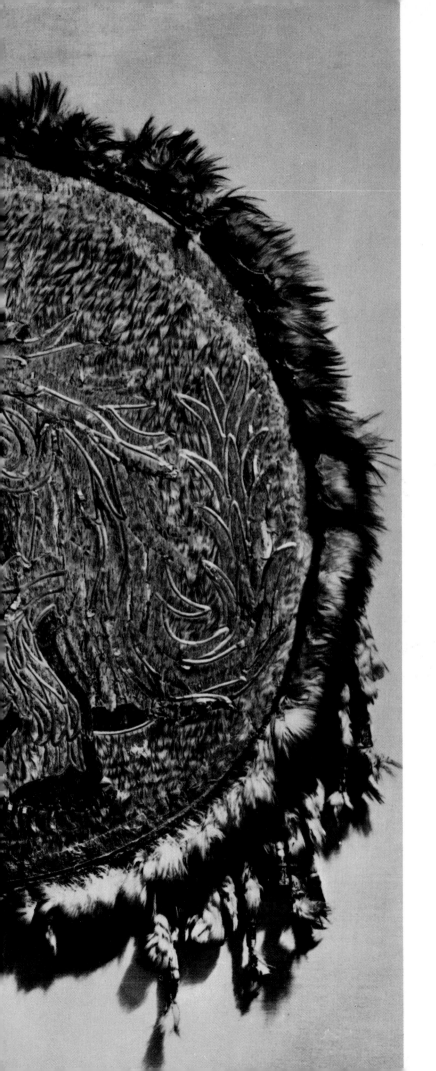

THE LIFE
AND
TIMES OF

CORTÉS

PAUL HAMLYN

London·New York·Sydney·Toronto

WERE THE "CONQUISTADORES" HEROES OR ADVENTURERS?

Who were the *conquistadores*, or conquerors of Mexico, and what did they stand for? For four centuries historians have argued over the extraordinary feat of a handful of soldiers, completed by officials and missionaries, which gave Spain possession of almost the whole of what was then the New World. Two opposing views of it are held: the first sees the *conquistadores* as bigoted adventurers, urged on by their greed for gold; the second sees in the conquest a spirit of heroism, an altruistic devotion to the Catholic faith, the spirit the Spaniards had already shown during the "holy war" fought against the Moslems, which in January 1492 expelled them from their last stronghold, Granada. No doubt the truth lies somewhere between the two; the men who conquered the new world were a paradoxical mixture of piety and greed. The Catholic Kings, Ferdinand and Isabella, were responsible for the reconquest, and during their reign they changed the whole face of Spain. Like Portugal, Spain was the natural gateway to the New World, which was discovered in 1492, the very same year that the Moslems were finally expelled from Spain. But the Portuguese looked for India by sailing round Africa and it was only later, quite by chance, that the Portuguese Cabral discovered Brazil. The Catholic Kings' navigators, on the other hand, sailed by a "direct" westward route, towards a continent they thought was the legendary Cipango, described by Marco Polo and thought to be enormously rich and highly civilised. Spanish culture was then at its height: freed at last from their debt to the Moslems, literature and the arts were flourishing in a revival of national consciousness. The sea routes were open, in what seemed a spirit of noble competitiveness with the Portuguese. In every port preparations were made for long voyages: dockyards rang with carpenters' hammers, sailmakers made sails tough enough to withstand the force of the wind in unknown seas, cartographers made maps based on information from old travellers and merchants. Spain needed gold: it had been bled by the long war against the Moslems, who left magnificent buildings behind but took all the gold and valuables they could carry with them beyond the Straits of Gibraltar. Spain needed navigators, soldiers and a great empire.

Left hand page: Queen Isabella and Ferdinand the Catholic, from a bas-relief in the choir of San Benito et Real, at Vasco de la Zerza, now in the Vallodolid Museum. This page, top left: Isabella's crown, now in Toledo Catheral; top right: the arms of the Catholic kings, whom Spaniards call simply "the kings".

Below: Map of the western Mediterranean, with the Iberian peninsula stretching well out into the great unknown ocean, where Spaniards and Portuguese competed against one another. The Spaniards colonised almost the whole of the New World, except for Brazil, discovered on April 25, 1500 by the Portuguese Cabral.

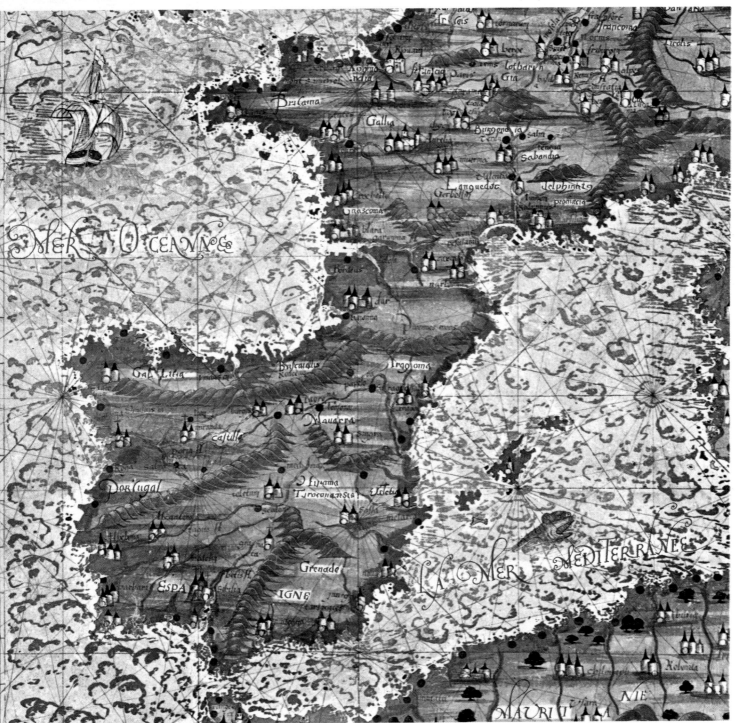

A PAGE IN HISTORY WAITING TO BE WRITTEN

By his epic journey, Christopher Columbus changed the historical outlook of the known world; he landed in a new country that was still entirely undiscovered. Spain in particular was stimulated by his discovery, and seemed to feel that man was on the brink of a new age. Infinite wealth lay beyond the ocean, awaiting those bold enough to cross it, while at home glory and honour awaited them on their return. Historical tradition tells us that those whose horizons at home were limited by the life they led in office or barracks were drawn to the new world by the thought of gold, glory and the gospel. Any Spaniard who could read and write would have preferred to spend his life in a white house in Hispaniola (the present-day Haiti) or Cuba, even if it still meant poring over accounts in a dusty office, for it was a way of escaping the dreariness of home. And besides, everyone was quite certain that one day his luck would turn, that he would get his chance to escape from paperwork, maybe to fight or to govern a province,

or even to hold the cross on high. In any case, across the ocean there was an enormous country still to be explored, peopled by "noble savages", ignorant men who were stunned by everything that had landed on their shores. They could not weave or make pottery, had no domestic animals (later, the Spaniards were amazed by what they found on the broad highlands), were gentle and ready to do the humblest work: Columbus had said so. In exchange for glass beads and red caps, they had submitted to him and brought him supplies of all kinds. There seemed little point, now, in sweating out a harsh existence in Castille or Andalusia, in Estremadura or Leon, where there was precious little chance of advancement. But now the Spanish armies were carrying war and conquest right into Africa, where the *Moriscos* wept like women, remembering the proud cities they had been unable to defend like men, as the mother of the last caliph of Granada put it. Spain was passing through what we would now call a boom of colonial expansion. Columbus had turned a great page in the book of history and the Spaniards had a completely blank one before them, waiting for what they would write on it. Young noblemen, university students, the clerks that swarmed in the office of every notary and lawyer in Spain were straining to be off. Even the Church encouraged the idea of colonisation, demanding that the faith should be spread with missionary fervour among the pagan natives of the new world.

Left: allegory depicting Christopher Columbus presenting the new world and its riches to the enthroned Catholic kings. Painting by Antonio Gonzalez y Velazquez in the Museum of Fine Arts at Quimper. The discovery of America brought an unprecedented wave of euphoria in Spain, although later on the flood of gold brought economic havoc. Below: an old map showing the first of the new lands discovered by the Spaniards across the ocean; they appear in it as islands. The Antilles, in the Caribbean, were in fact the first to be discovered, Columbus himself making his first landing on an island he called San Salvador.

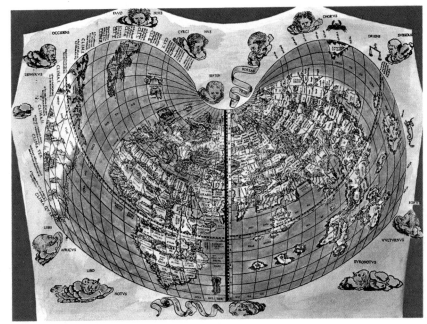

Left: portraits of Christopher Columbus (in the Palazzo Tursi in Genoa) and of Magellan, from a 16th-century engraving. Columbus was the first man who dared cross the ocean in search of the country he thought was Cipango, which Marco Polo had mentioned, but the Portuguese Magellan was the first to set off (in 1519) in an effort to sail right round the world. He was killed in the Philippines. Columbus and Magellan were two of the world's greatest navigators and opened the way for Cortés. Columbus made his journey because he clung tenaciously to the belief that he could reach the Indies by going west, and Magellan set out to discover whether the Philippines were in the part of the world which Alexander VI had assigned to Spain.

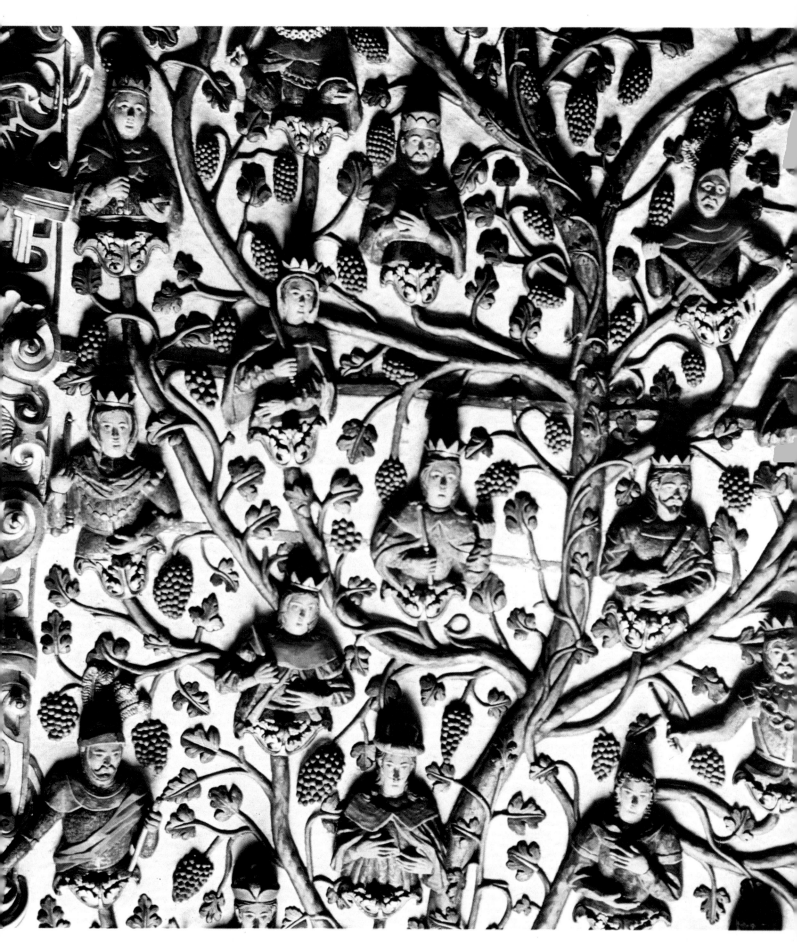

8

A FEW SUPERMEN AND AN ARMY OF OFFICIALS

The *conquistadores'* achievement was not really weighed up until the nineteenth century, when some Spanish researchers went back to the original sources to see whether their chief detractors, Las Casas and his followers, had based their attacks upon what actually happened. But it was romanticism that was really drawn to the idea of the conquest and those who had taken part in it. Nietzsche, Ibsen, D'Annunzio, Kipling and many others, although they did not go deeply into the matter, fed this interest: Cortés and his desperate followers seemed to embody the figure of the white man as an "inevitable" superman: Jack London, too, with his deterministic outlook, saw them as such. They seemed really god-like, *teúles* as the Aztecs called them. But in reading the accounts of them and going back to the original sources, it is odd to find that their power lay not in their weapons, nor in their political ability, nor even in their personal influence. What kept them in power was the army of lawyers, clerks and bureaucrats that was ever at hand during the American adventures – if not during the actual fighting then immediately afterwards, as soon as the conquest was achieved. Adventurers like Cortés were involved in all the complexities of the law, restricted in all they did by a bewildering array of permissions and prohibitions, laws, warnings and concessions made in the name of king and of Christ, who sometimes seemed like a mere civil servant himself. The Spanish crown distrusted the rather maverick spirit of the explorers, and feared that, if left to themselves, they would become a new feudal nobility, paying only lip service to the king of Spain. It was during the conquest of America that Spanish bureaucracy, which had first entangled Columbus in its toils, really grew and flourished. Neither Cortés nor Balboa, one of the greatest of the Spanish explorers, who was finally hanged by his own men, managed to escape it. Cortés in particular had the most religious respect for law and order, acquired, very likely, in his 'prentice years in lawyers' offices in Vallodolid, or in the cold lecture halls of Salamanca university where lawyers were trained. Everyone agreed that in dealing with the king of Spain – Charles V – Cortés wrote and behaved like a clerk or a notary. He tried to act within the framework of the law.

CORTÉS WAS NOT A PLUNDERER AND THE AZTECS WERE NOT "NOBLE SAVAGES"

The idea of the *conquistadores* as bloodthirsty plunderers – called by some historians the "black legend", because of the sombre colours in which they have been painted – found support, both at the time and later, in books like the *Relacion de la destruccion de las Indias*, written by the Dominican Bartolomeo de las Casas in 1552. He had lost hope of seeing the new laws for the protection of the natives applied – laws he himself had put forward in Spain. The chroniclers of the conquest in the second half of the 16th century and in the 17th, such as the friar Agostine Calancla, the friar Mautia de San Martin, the bishop Pedro de Iza, and Torribio de Benavente, criticised the *conquistadores* not so much for demolishing the pagan temples or forcing the natives to be converted, as for exploiting the entire population and reducing it to slavery. Later, however, the English puritans and the French of the eighteenth-century cared not so much about their ill-treatment of the natives as for the fact that they had pitilessly overthrown the ancient institutions and religions of the pre-conquest America. The fact is that men like Hernan Cortés or Francisco Pizarro – who in any case differed as much as a 16th century gentleman could from an illiterate swineherd – cannot be understood without an understanding of the conquest. Their hostile critics suppressed and ignored every incident that revealed faith or altruism, civility or understanding throughout the conquest on either side, forgetting that Cortés was fundamentally a just man, morally sound, and even according to his lights a humane man. As he followed a destiny which he believed to be God's will, Cortés showed none of Pizarro's cold cruelty. He conquered Mexico but tried to understand the Mexicans; he captured Montezuma, the emperor-god, but as far as we know he was not responsible for his tragic end. Certainly the *conquistadores* were hungry for gold and land, but so were the Aztecs against whom they fought. If the Spaniards were sometimes bloodthirsty the Aztecs were hardly less so. Moreover, there was a desperate heroism about the men who marched through the hostile countryside towards an extraordinary and unknown kingdom. Cortés was not merely a plunderer, and the Aztecs he met on his progress were not "noble savages".

Left-hand page top: a map of the Gulf of Mexico, with the north on the right, as is indicated by the compass card in the centre of the Gulf. Cortés was a man of honour and his adventures in Mexico always kept a certain adventurous flavour about them, whereas Pizarro (in the engraving, below, left) was violent and bloodthirsty and conquered Peru (opposite page, below right: an old map) through treachery and deception. Pizarro was an illiterate swineherd, whereas Cortés had spent two years at the university at Salamanca and had worked in a lawyer's office. The civilization the Spaniards found in Mexico was an unexpected gift to the whole of humanity, for the Mexicans cultivated plants and raised animals that were unknown in Europe. But what most astonished the explorers were the remarkable buildings in the squares of the cities of central America.
Above: the pyramid of the Adivino (that is, of the wizard). Left: the characteristic arrow-shaped door of the governor's palace at Uxmal. Today virgin forest surrounds many of the ancient Mexican buildings.

FIVE LETTERS TO CHARLES V, ACCOMPANIED BY PRECIOUS GIFTS

In his letters to Charles V Cortés wrote directly of the conquest. There are five of them, rather long-winded, as was usual at the time, but full of interesting details, and if we read between the lines they reveal a great deal about Cortés' thoughts and feelings. The first letter introduces the queen, Joan the Mad, and her son the emperor Charles V, to the impressive sight of Yucatan and Mexico. Cortés is still seeing them with a certain sense of awe, and his style in the letter is rather dull and heavy; its legal, churchy air has made more than one critic remark on the fact that Cortés never completely freed himself of the language he had learnt in the service of the Spanish bureaucracy, both at home and overseas. Yet it seems unlikely that a man as shrewd and intelligent as Cortés should suddenly, in his second letter, alter his literary style. This second letter, a long one written when he had already met Montezuma and Tenochtitlan had been conquered, destroyed and then rebuilt, is a masterpiece, a portrait in colour of a king and a people, superior even to those left us by Díaz del Castillo and other chroniclers. So it is probable that in his first letter Cortés used the legal-sounding style to show the king (and in a way to stress the fact) that Veracruz had been founded and the decision to march against the Aztec capital without Velazquez's authorisations taken quite legally, by obeying pre-arranged orders and recording everything in the necessary documents. Thus he increased his own responsibility (but also his own power), diminished the power of the governor of Cuba in the eyes of the king, and gave honour to the reigning house. Cortés now knew he could seize Montezuma's kingdom. The five letters he wrote were addressed directly to the king and accompanied by gifts of gold and precious metals. The Aztecs did not lay any great importance on gold as their economy was not built on it – jade and turquoise were far more valuable, and silver, because it was comparatively rare, may have been the most prized of all. But to Cortés gold meant power and fame. The Spaniards melted down many of the beautiful ornaments they captured, but the first trophies astounded Albrecht Dürer when he saw them in 1520, and made him declare that the hundreds and thousands of florins they were worth were nothing compared to the joy inspired by such wonderful work.

For thousands of years the Mexican world had been unknown in Europe: when the Spaniards lifted the veil from the scene they were astonished. The "noble savages" were wonderful sculptors and builders, knew how to measure time and lived in a highly organised society. Left hand page: human head in stone, in the National Anthropological Museum in Mexico City, which, in spite of the fact that works of art flowed out unchecked to Europe for decades, contains the finest art of central America. Archaeological digs are regularly made in the most famous sites. This page top left: the pyramid of Tajin, near Veracruz, which shows how magnificently the pre-Conquest builders worked. Top right: details of an Aztec codex, showing Mexicans building a pyramid. Below: scene on a painted drum: warriors and peasants dance in a ring, with a drummer and another musician with a percussion instrument in the centre. The Mexicans danced a great deal as a part of their religion and painted their faces to do so.

THE IRRESISTIBLE CALL TO ADVENTURE

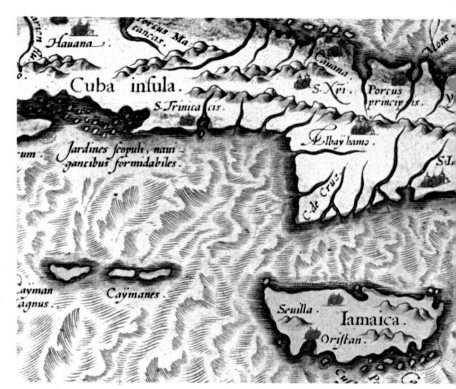

Hernan Cortés was born at Medellin in Estremadura, in 1485, the son of Don Martin who had served the king of Castile and now enjoyed a small income, and Doña Catalina, a devout woman. He grew up at a time in which Spain, having emerged from the clutches of Islam, was living adventurously, dreaming of a great empire. Every Spanish boy thought romantically of the conquest of Granada and the final expulsion of the Moslems, the occupation of the Canary Isles, the first exploits in Africa, and Columbus' voyage. On the ships that crossed the ocean fifteen-year-olds enrolled with mature adventurers, all seeking a new life. In 1499 Hernan was sent to study at Salamanca, the most famous Spanish university, but after two years he vanished, reappearing later in Valladolid, in a notary's office, where hunger had clearly driven him. It seems that later he tried to reach Italy to seek his fortune (this was the golden age of the Renaissance); but at nineteen we find him already embarked for the new world. In 1504, in fact, he landed at San Domingo, the Antilles island Columbus had named Hispaniola. What he did there at first we do not know; very likely he worked as a clerk, for the Spanish conquest was marking time. The early *conquistadores* had realised that the gold was not found in its natural state lying about the countryside, and that the Indians would often defend their land and villages tenaciously, even with their lives. In those years the Spanish crown showed little interest in the world discovered by Columbus, because its apparent advantages seemed far fewer than those Columbus had promised. Officials were now taking over: these were the king's men, who declared themselves "bound to the orders of the king our lord", and flung Indians, peasants or admirals into prison if the distant king heard the smallest rumour or suspicion of disobedience. But Cortés could not bear to toil in the sunny offices of Hispaniola: he saw the sea and the hills, stretching out as far as he could see, hiding unknown horizons, unknown chances of success, mysterious places where people he might conquer must live. A twentieth-century man, living in an age when there are no hidden lands to discover, can only imagine the excitement Cortés must have felt. America seemed as remote as the moon. The very breath of the sea kept him awake at night.

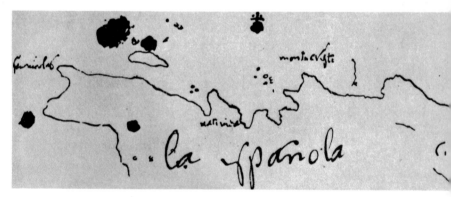

Above: map of the Antilles in the Museum of America in Madrid, showing Puerto Rico (San Juan), Hispaniola (Haiti), Jamaica and Cuba, and some smaller islands. Santa Domingo in Hispaniola was Cortés' first experience of the New World. Opposite page: the outline of Hispaniola, attributed to Columbus. Below left: part of the university of Salamanca, where Hernan Cortés studied, and from which it seems he fled to try to reach Italy. Below: middle left hand page: a striking portrait of the future conqueror of Mexico. This page left: Titian's painting of the emperor Charles V now in the Prado, Madrid. Cortés sent several letters to the king of Spain, written in very bureaucratic style, yet giving much valuable information about the conquest of Montezuma's kingdom. This page below: one of the buildings in the heart of the central American forest: the temple of the Jaguars at Chichen Itza. Cortés was not indifferent to Mexican civilisation: indeed, his letter shows his warm response to it. He was always fascinated by it and always felt great liking for the people he had conquered, respecting their great sense of discipline, their state organisations and their military prowess.

15

This page below: the hilt of the sword Cortés used during the conquest of Mexico, preserved in the Royal Armoury of Madrid. Cortés was loved by his soldiers for his bravery in combat and for his great sense of justice. On many occasions his example and his rousing words turned the tide of battle. Right: an engraving showing Cortés in the feathered helmet, with Gonzalo Sandoval, one of his most trusted officers. Cortés always made good use of his own officers and gave them military and political missions, sending them on embassies to the interior. Politically he was remarkably shrewd.

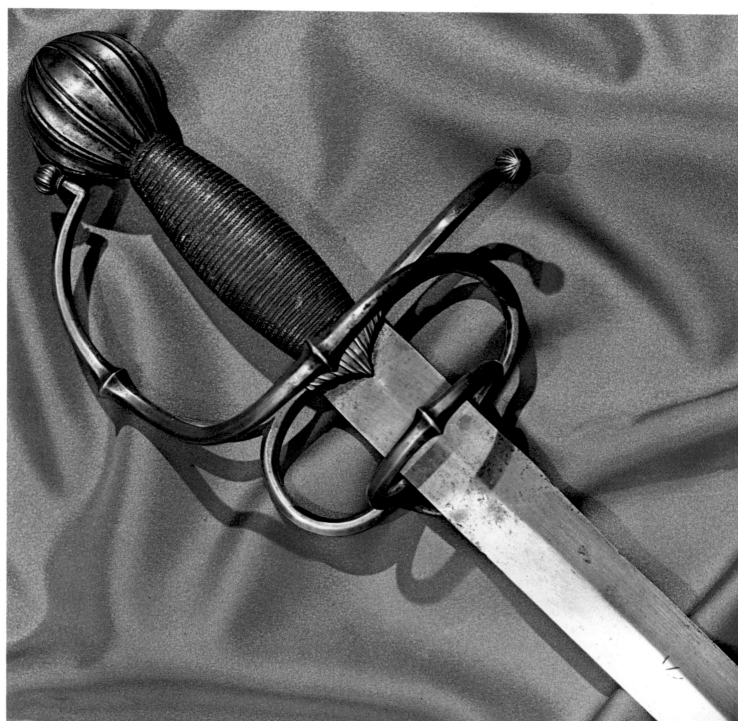

A KINDLY SPIRIT HARDENED BY THE DEMANDS OF STATE

This page top: a stretch of beach not far from where Cortés' expedition, which the Cuban governor Diego Valazquez thought was to be merely exploratory, set sail. Below: a woodcut of Spanish ships. Those used by Cortés were long and narrow, with a light draught that would allow a good watch to be kept along the shore. There were two types of light fast ships: those called lateens because they had lateen sails on every mast, and those called round ships, which had square sails, the main mast for'ard and new rigging and pulley blocks to sail close-hauled, that is to sail close to unfavourable winds.

Everyone who knew Cortés, even those who had little liking for him, like Father Las Casas, were struck by the nobility of his manners, as well as by his undeniable shrewdness. Those five or six years of complete obscurity at Santa Domingo must have contained some incident that brought the young clerk to the notice of Diego Velazquez, a powerful man who had followed Columbus to the New World and was also a friend of the second admiral of the ocean, Diego Columbus. In fact it was Diego Columbus who had given him Cuba, the largest island of the Antilles, to colonise. We do not know how or when Cortés and Velazquez met. We know that Cortés was a pleasant, witty man; he did all he could to make friends and to keep them, and always treated them generously; he sought the friendship of the best and most distinguished, admired those who had shown courage, despised the cowardly and the weak, and honoured the old. His contemporary, Cervantes de Salazar, tells us this, and Bernal Díaz del Castillo, a brave soldier who described the Mexican conquest, confirms it. Díaz says that even in the moments of anger Cortés never lost his good manners, and never cursed or swore; that when he was crossed a vein in his neck and another in his forehead swelled up, but he never spoke. Anyone who spoke offensively in his presence was told "Be silent and go with God. Mind what you say or I shall have you punished." Díaz also tells us that Cortés had twice been elected mayor of the town in which he lived, an honour which is a good indication of his popularity. There is no doubt that the hard years at Valladolid and Salamanca and his long service at Santa Domingo had taught him patience, but they had also made him burningly ambitious. His innate kindliness was undoubtedly hardened by his clerical work, by all the corrupt practices and injustices he saw done daily to the colonists, the soldiers and the Indians. The grasping landowners saw the native islanders as their slaves, to be worked until they died of illness or exhaustion, and then to be replaced by captives from the Bahamas, or luckless negroes imported from the Portuguese possessions in West Africa. We must remember however, that disregard for human life was common in the sixteenth century: the punishments meted out to criminals and heretics in Spain remind us of this.

CORTÉS IS GIVEN COMMAND OF AN EXPEDITION

Diego Velazquez, the governor of Cuba, was willy nilly extremely important to what Cortés was doing. During the colonisations of the largest of the Antilles, Cortés quite suddenly became prominent when, in 1512, he played an important part in the foundation of Santiago de Baracoa, there obtaining land and *reparta-mientos de indios* (a kind of reserve with a right of exploitation). All at once we see the young man turned from a clerk into a landowner and stock breeder. By then, no one in Cuba deluded himself that there was gold in abundance; indeed, there were no gold mines on the islands, only fertile soil where the sugar cane that is still its main product grew wonderfully. Velazquez was no *conquistador*: he was a merchant above all, a shrewd, cunning business man. In military terms he could be called a quartermaster, good at

provisioning sea voyages and providing supplies of clothes and food, for which the soldiers he had sent out exploring had to pay him dearly. According to Bartolomeo de las Casas, Cortés was very servile towards Velazquez until he obtained an important position. How true this is, it is hard to say today; but we do know that Cortés did anything he could to be sent to "the mainland", that is to the American conti-nent. There it was a case not of finding land to be farmed, as in Cuba, but of encountering a warlike people that had built cities and possessed enormous wealth. All kinds of legends were circulating about America, many of them the fantastic products of the explorer's imagination. Cortés' dream as a youngster had, now that he was thirty-four, turned into a burning desire. All he cared about was the provisioning of ships with food, weapons, bags of powder and horses – which were extremely valuable animals. He flung himself completely into preparing for the journey, and Diego Velazquez, partly because he would get large sums of gold out of it, approved his plan for the voyage and his idea of landing in the area explored the previous year by Juan de Grijalba, also acting under Velazquez's orders.

Those who first cultivated and colonized the larger islands of the Antilles were drawn there by the thought of the civilisations which they believed flourished on the still mysterious continent of America. It was said that pyramids larger than those of Egypt arose along the coast (the photograph on the left-hand page shows a typical building at El Tajin) and in every port ships were equipped to explore the coast of the Gulf of Mexico. Above left: detail of a shipbuilding scene. Top right: woodcut of Spanish ship of the 15th century sailing with wind astern and mainsail billowing. Below: map of the sea of the Antilles.

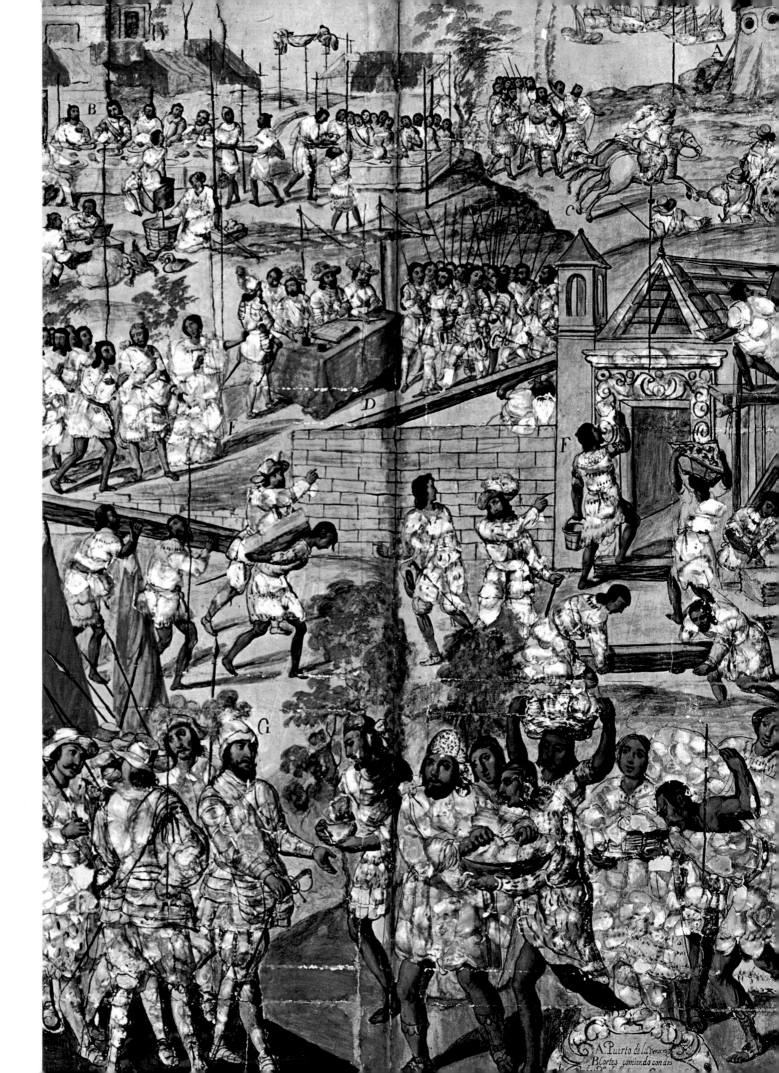

A Puerto de la Veracruz
B Cortes comiendo con dos

VASCO NUNEZ DE BALBOA WAS HIS MODEL

Left-hand page: scenes from the history of the Conquest, from a large painting in the Museum of America in Madrid. High up on the right is the port of Veracruz, on the Mexican coast; on the left, Cortés is feasting with some ambassadors who have arrived from inland districts; in the centre, the Villa Rica de Vera Cruz is being built; at the bottom Cortés enters a village where he is offered gifts and slaves. This page above: a map of the Isthmus of Panama, in the War Ministry in Paris. Below: encircled, a portrait of Vasco Nunez de Balboa, who was the first to see the Pacific.

When we consider carefully Cortés' design to reach the American mainland and there undertake one of the most hazardous conquests in the history of the exploration of America, we discover that he was preceded by another expedition, to which most historians have given little attention. This was the journey of Vasco Nunez de Balboa, which led to the discovery of the Pacific. Balboa was quite unknown when he set sail secretly with a troop of soldiers which landed on the mainland to help a Spanish garrison which was in danger. And yet, when faced with difficulties, his qualities became clear – personal courage, diplomatic ability, patience in dealing with native leaders, and a capacity to please the crown by writing long detailed letters to the king in Spain: all qualities later found in Cortés. Indeed, one might say that Cortés was Balboa's model pupil, and that both men came close to the Renaissance ideal of a man. It is to the honour of them both that they were, basically, acting for military reasons, and that at the same time they cared for the social conditions of those who depended on them, whether as soldiers or as slaves. They were both a long way from the small-minded men who represented the Spanish crown in its American colonies and whose thoughts turned only to the furthering of their own interests. The historian Oviedo tells us that "outstanding men and leaders came out of the school of Vasco Nunez" and there is no doubt that many incidents and Cortés' behaviour in various circumstances were inspired by Balboa's conduct on his journey to the Pacific. While he was governor of Castilla de Oro, on the north east coast of what is now the Isthmus of Panama, Balboa heard from the natives that there was a great sea to the west. So he set off with 190 Spaniards and, on the hills of Darien, had the privilege of being the first white man to see the Pacific Ocean, which he named the Southern Sea. This discovery stimulated those European merchants who hoped to find a sea route westward to India and as Cortés entered Mexico Magellan set sail for the east. Balboa cleared the coastal forest, built villages and introduced farming, but jealous enemies turned the king against him. He was replaced as governor of the territory by Pedro Arias de Avila, who had him summarily tried and executed in 1519.

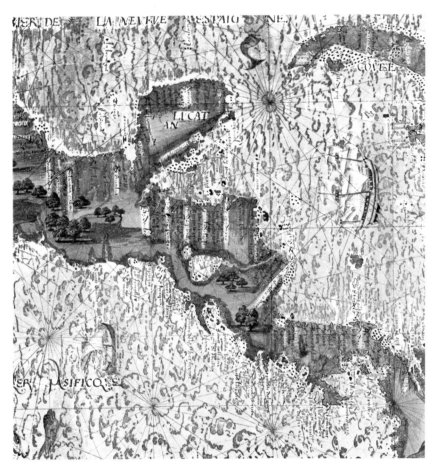

21

CORTÉS' FOLLOWERS MAKE HIM CAPTAIN GENERAL

On February 10, 1519, Cortés and his army set sail from Cuba: 508 soldiers, 100 sailors and 16 horses. Their weapons, apart from the ship's cannons, consisted of flint-locks, arquebuses and even bows, and when they first landed by the River Tabasco these proved immediately effective when the natives, who proved to be anything by gentle and primitive, were in no way frightened by the Spaniards. It was after his victory over the people of Tabasco that the local chiefs presented themselves to Cortés, offering him rich gifts in token of peace, among them women, which he shared out among his officers. One of these women, baptised with the name of Marina, was later to become his own adviser and interpreter and to play an important part in his struggle against the Aztecs. Cortés then turned north. On Maundy Thursday he took the land where Veracruz stands today. This district was already under Aztec rule and the following day messengers from the emperor Montezuma asked to be received. When they left they took messages from Cortés to their emperor. A week later they were back, but with a negative answer. Although he sent gold and precious stones, Montezuma refused to welcome Cortés. Diego Velazquez's orders were to explore and exchange goods, whereas Cortés wanted to deal directly with the head of an empire he already knew was enormous. He was now beginning to think of going beyond the mountains. Many of his officers agreed with him while others still felt bound by the orders of the governor of Cuba. The decisive turn came when his officers appointed Cortés captain-general and chief justice of the city they founded there, called Villa Rica de la Vera Cruz. Cortés now depended on the king of Spain for the authority he needed.

Left hand page top: a Spanish squadron sets sail from the Cuban port of Santiago. Below left: large portrait of Hernan Cortés in the Museum of America in Madrid. Right: Mexican boat, in an old engraving. This page top left: Cortés receives the gifts sent to him by Montezuma on his landing in Mexico.

Top right: engraving showing the emperor Montezuma in rather strange clothes. Immediately above: Aztec miniature depicting a battle between Mexicans and Spanish sailors who have landed from a ship that is anchored, but still has its sails unfurled, ready to set off in case of trouble. Left: nineteenth-century painting of an episode in the journey of Juan de Grijalba to the River Tabasco, a year before Cortés' coming – a journey which spurred the governor of Cuba on to organise further expeditions to explore the shores of the mysterious continent. Diego Velazquez cannot have had the least idea that one of these excursions, that of Hernan Cortés, would lead to the conquest of the greatest empire in the whole of Central and North America. One of Cortés' biographers who wrote about his enterprise, Bernal Díaz del Castillo, had also taken part in Grijalba's expedition and was very free with advice to his new leader. We are indebted to Díaz for his vivid first-hand account of these early voyages of exploration.

This page below: one of the crosses set up by the Spaniards along the road from Veracruz to the Mexican Capital. This page right: Cortés in the centre, wearing a plumed helmet, receives Montezuma's envoys; at the top of the picture the sinking of the ships on August 15 1519, and the start of the march to the interior.

Right hand page above: Diego Velazquez appoints Cortés as leader of the expedition; and below: Cortés hides the materials saved from the sunken ships. After leaving Sanlucar de Barrameda, Cortés, son of a modest captain, spent several undistinguished years in Cuba. In 1511, with Velazquez, he took part in the conquest of the island. As a criado, that is one of the governor's followers, he was taken on as secretary and treasurer, receiving a repartamiento of slaves and grants of land. This did not prevent him plotting against Velazquez, as far as we know, but a short period of isolation was his only punishment. In spite of this Velazquez bore him no ill-will, although he might have been justified in doing so; he had confidence in Cortés and chose him to command the new expedition.

CORTÉS SINKS HIS SHIPS AND MAKES RETURN IMPOSSIBLE

After the expedition's notary had ratified the fact that Cortés had been named captain-general, the largest ship in the fleet set sail for Spain, laden with gold and other valuables, which the Spaniards sent as gifts to King Charles to gain his confidence and show him that Cortés and his expedition deserved the crown's esteem and approval. Cortés also made the newly appointed magistrates of Veracruz give him a new commission, to justify his arrogant flouting of Velazquez, and sent to the king for confirmation of it. At this point, those who supported Velazquez tried to rise up against Cortés, but a spy told him all about it and betrayed his companions, who were very harshly treated. This brought Cortés to a decision which even today arouses arguments among historians. He had all the iron nails, ropes, and weapons taken from the ships, and then sank them, every one. Escape was now impossible, and all the Spaniards could do was march on Tenochtitlan, Montezuma's great city, which they had been hearing about for so long. Was it an act of defiant heroism, or merely cold calculation, for Cortés to deprive himself of his only link with the old world, with Cuba and Hispaniola, with Trinidad and Spain itself? The legend of Cortés' self-confidence, of the way he was predestined to conquer, was born from this action of his. When Cervantes made Don Quixote cite the greatest acts of heroism in the history of the world, he included among them, as the single modern episode among many other illustrations taken from ancient times, this action of Cortés. Nevertheless, Cortés destroyed his ships out of absolute necessity, not in the hope of glory or in order to defy the governors of Cuba and Santo Domingo but because it was the only way in which he could fulfill his plans. With Velazquez's supporters silenced, the astounded soldiers could do nothing but set off across the mountains in search of Eldorado and the sailors, willy-nilly, had to join them. Only thus can Cortés' action be judged and explained: it was a ruse that forced him and his officers – apart from the recalcitrant soldiers – to march in the only direction in which they thought there were food and riches for all, enough to make up for what they abandoned. The sinking of the ships was the die cast by Cortés when he crossed his own Rubicon.

HIS STRENGTH CAME FROM HIS OWN WEAKNESS

Cortés' violent act in sinking the ships cut the last and only link between his expedition and what was called the civilised world, and freed his officers and men from their longing to return and the uncertainty of what they were doing. But it did not free him, their leader, from his own responsibilities towards his king and in the face of history. In sinking the ships, was he acting on his own initiative or did someone urge or advise him to do it? This has yet to be established. But whether he acted reluctantly or with cold determination, it was the beginning of the dramatic events in which Cortés was at once both protagonist and scapegoat. Probably he had never felt so much alone, however firm his decision, as when he gave that order. This is clear from Díaz del Castillo's chronicle, which first attributes the idea to some of Cortés' most devoted officers, but later says that when they suggested the idea to him he said he had already thought of it, and had been unable to make up his mind. He wanted others to suggest it to him and, when he saw they agreed with him, felt a sense of liberation. The first step was taken when some of the ship's captains came to tell him that the ships had become infested with ship-worm and were unusable. So the small band of soldiers was reinforced by the sailors who had to disembark. In his report to the king Cortés said nothing about this episode: he knew he had not gone by the rules and that, as Velazquez's friends said, it was all "irregular". Having destroyed the ships, he spoke to the men and told them that their only hope now lay in God; then he repeated Julius Caesar's words when he crossed the Rubicon: "The die is cast". What did his officers really think? Did they have confidence in what he was doing? At this distance in time it is hard to tell. We know for certain of Cortés' own unshakeable faith, but also of his sense of loneliness when he set off on horseback up the harsh rocky landscape of the plateau, not knowing what lay ahead and seeing no very favourable future there. Yet he advanced quickly, and showing gifts possessed only by the greatest adventurers, managed to get most of his men facing up to whatever happened however unexpected and unfavourable it might be. He managed to create strength even from weakness, his own weakness and that of his men, and this was surely a heroic achievement.

Left hand page: "Cortés' Pass", a plain that opens up between the harsh mountains the Spaniards climbed on their way from the coast to the Mexican capital. This page below left: in this painting in the American museum in Madrid, three Spanish officials are looking at Mexican idols offered the butchered bodies of human victims. Above: two Mexicans harshly tortured by the Spaniards. In the year that Cortés landed in the New World, Isabella the Catholic died in Spain. In her will, the great queen left these noble words: "The King my Lord, the Princess my daughter, and the Prince my son shall allow no Indians living of the islands and the mainland to suffer harm, either in their persons or in their possessions. They must see to it that these people are treated with justice and kindness". Pizarro committed savage crimes, but Cortés was also accused of great cruelty. Admittedly he was sometimes cruel, but only when forced by the situation to be so. We must not forget, either, that torture and suffering were then current, even in Renaissance Europe. And certainly the ferocious religious rites of the Aztecs were no very edifying example.

CORTÉS CLEVERLY EXPLOITS RIVALRIES AMONG THE MEXICANS

The civilization the Spaniards found was profoundly different from any they had known so far. The gods were terrible and demanded human victims. These included Xiuhtecutli, god of fire, and the spectral Coatlicue, goddess of the earth and of fertility (opposite page). On the other hand, Aztec arts sometimes reached extraordinary heights. The Aztecs could weave and made delicate mosaics of feathers (this page, below). Bottom of page: Aztec miniature showing a battle scene between Spaniards and Aztecs, one of whom is dressed in a jaguar skin, which means he was one of the warriors of death.

Marching in from the coast the Spaniards reached Quiahuitzlan, a city on the edge of the high plateau, thirteen miles from the sea. Among the many Totonacs living in that district, they met five Aztec tax collectors, very richly dressed in embroidered cloaks and loincloths, who were walking along holding bunches of flowers in their hands and followed by slaves waving huge fans to keep off the flies. They ignored Cortés. When the Spaniards arrived some of the Totonacs had helpfully brought them food and drink. The five Aztecs considered this grave insubordination, and as a punishment tried to sacrifice twenty youths and girls. Cortés' reaction to this was violent: he flung the five haughty officials into prison. The Totonacs were divided into several parties: some realised that the arrival of the Spaniards would at last allow them to shake off the Aztec yoke: others maintained, sensibly enough, that they would be going from bad to worse. And here Cortés showed another of his abilities – his diplomacy and persuasive power. By the way he behaved he seemed to be reviving the classic Roman idea of divide and rule, which, in that hostile country so immensely far from all European customs and forms of logic, must have been rather hard to put into effect. But he was helped, as we shall see, by the delicate artistry of his interpreter, Doña Marina. In his *Cartas de relacion*, that is, the letter he sent to the Spanish crown, Cortés was later to explain how cleverly he exploited the ideas of a minority to make this minority his friend and ally: but later on, for political reasons, he made even the most faithful tribes submit to the rule of Spain, and although he gave his allies responsibilities they were more high-sounding than real. Just as Caesar used the tribes of central Gaul to fight against the other tribes, so Cortés cunningly split the enemy side into rival bands, in order to weaken them all, and this ruse succeeded perfectly. His report is, of course, prejudiced and limited, and some things are very subjectively described, but Díaz del Castillo's splendid book shows the leader and his follower each confirming what the other said. Lopez de Gomara, Cortés' friend and chaplain, kept a diary as well, but it is prejudiced and gives a rather meagre amount of information. It is Díaz del Castillo who writes most vividly.

DONA MARINA, AN INDIAN, WAS HIS FINEST HELPER

Among the young Indian women given to Cortés as soon as he landed on the coast, one who was baptised as Marina became the most useful interpreter the Spaniards could have found. As Cortés' adviser she tried to improve relations between the invaders and her own people. This page below: a scene in which the young women are offered to the Spaniards. Below that: Cortés with Marina, and more Indian women given to the Spaniards. Opposite page, above: the gay welcome given by the Aztecs to the first Spaniards they met. Below: a Mexican chief, Xiloteca, bringing chieftain's daughters.

It seems fairly clear what Cortés had in mind when, at night, he freed two of the Aztec officials imprisoned at Quiahuitzlan, and sent them secretly to their emperor Montezuma: he meant that they should tell him of the stranger's clemency. The Totonacs, although they knew he had freed the prisoners, made no efforts to understand his attitude, and in fact gave him men for his army. In these early diplomatic manoeuvres with Montezuma's officials and his subjects, the young Indian girl who had been given to Cortés when he landed at Tabasco and whom he had at first handed over to one of his officers, began to matter. This was Marina, daughter of chieftains, who spoke both Nahuatl, the Aztec's language, and that of the people along the coast; and she soon learnt Spanish quite easily. Marina was intelligent and no doubt in love with Cortés. She became his shadow, acting as his interpreter with the upland tribes, discovering a dangerous ambush laid by the Cholulans, softening the attitude of Montezuma when he was virtually a prisoner yet still powerful among his own people; it was she who told Cortés about the rivalries among the tribes, she who suggested the political plan of co-operating with those who were in revolt against the Aztecs. Though Indian women had certain rights as wives and mothers, their position in a polygamous society was not especially exalted, except perhaps among the Aztec nobles. This makes her behaviour all the more remarkable. The Aztecs understood her importance so well that they called the Spaniards *Malinche,* which meant Malina's men. Díaz del Castillo was quite firm when he said: "Doña Marina was very important in our conquest". Some historians think of her simply as Cortés' mistress, and think this explains her whole behaviour, which puts her on a level with any number of Indian women who sold themselves to men of another race. But if we read the reports of those who followed the expedition, we must realise that her presence had a special importance, even when she still belonged to Alonzo Puertocarrero, and then to Juan Jarmillo. Although she might appear to be a slave she was always at Cortés' side, advising him and giving him the benefit of her experience, that of a woman brought up in the Mexican culture of the mysterious Totonacs.

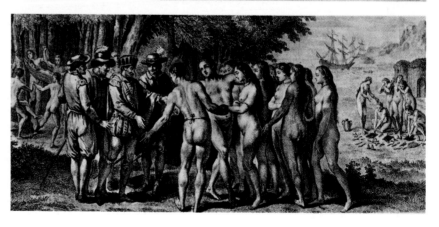

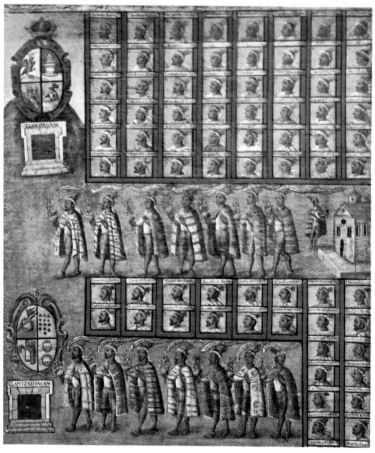

IN SIGHT OF THE CAPITAL

Opposite page above: view of Tenochtitlan, in the middle of its lake (19th-century print). Below left: chieftains of Tlaxala, 18th-century oil painting at the National Historical museum in Mexico City. Below right: meeting between the Spanish ambassadors and the Tlaxcalan rulers. This page below: Cortés and his followers enter Tenochtitlan (detail of panels on the Conquest), while the Mexicans gaze bewilderedly from their canoes at the horses, which were completely unknown to them and made the invaders look like monsters, half man, half horse. Horses, as well as firearms, played a major part in Cortés' conquest.

As they climbed the terrible rocky slopes of the Mexican highlands, the Spaniards reached the land of Tlaxcala. The Tlaxcalans were a noble and proud people who had submitted to the Aztecs but for some time had been filled with revolutionary ideas. At first they fought the Spaniards in small skirmishes that almost put an end to their advance – indeed they even thought of abandoning it as impossible. Then Cortés, with Marina's help and after many efforts and long discussions, managed to persuade them to ally themselves with him, and to regain their freedom by fighting the Aztecs. His shrewd diplomacy led to what Montezuma feared most of all – civil war. The Spaniards marched on Cholula, an important key city, where they were made welcome. And here something unexpected happened. In the city's large main square Cortés gathered the chiefs, who came accompanied by several thousand unarmed men awaiting his decision. The warriors from Tlaxcala, gathered all round the square, began at a given moment to kill their rivals from Cholula. The dead ran into thousands. None of the Spaniards gave an account of this massacre; Díaz del Castillo merely mentioned it, but with unusual vagueness, saying that Montezuma had persuaded the city chiefs to prepare an ambush for Cortés and his officers, and that Cortés himself gave orders to prevent it by having some of the Cholula officials killed. The rest must have been done by the Tlaxcalans on their own initiative, for vengeance on their old enemies. In fact, it would appear that the plot was suggested to Cortés by Doña Marina, who must have revealed the secret ambush and suggested the massacre. Whatever really happened, all the Aztecs between Cholula and the capital Tenochtitlan were terrified by the incident and by what they heard of the burning of Cholula and the destruction of the temple of Quetzalcoatl. This allowed the Spaniards to reach the mountains that enclosed the shell-shaped lake Texcoco, on whose islands the Aztecs' capital was built. Montezuma sent rich presents as bribes to get them to turn back, but to no avail. Cortés' shrewdness, the vendettas that divided the nations which had submitted to Montezuma, and the advice of Doña Marina had in a short time brought thousands of Spaniards into the heart of Central America.

THE GODS' REPLY WAS TO LET IN THE WHITE KING-GOD

Below: two details of the rites with which the Mexicans opened up the breast of their sacrificial victims and pulled out the still beating heart, which they laid on the altar in the teocalli, that is, the House of God. Cortés tried (see large picture on the right) to destroy the idols.

In the hope of halting the advance of Cortés, Montezuma had increased these sacrifices in the last days before the Spaniard's arrival. But the plumed serpent, who according to the ancient prophecy had begun to reconquer his own kingdom, was not halted. A prophecy attributed these words to Quetzalcoatl: "I shall return in a year of the roses and establish my rule". 1519 was, to the Aztecs, a year of the roses, and Cortés was Quetzalcoatl.

After the massacre at Cholula, the way to Tenochtitlan was open and the band of 400 Spaniards advanced upon Mexico. Terror filled the Aztecs' subject-peoples, and Montezuma himself, after taking council with his priests, decided to throw open the city gates. Human victims were sacrificed to the gods; oracular signs showed that the strangers must be allowed to enter; yet Montezuma hesitated. The reason for his uncertainty lay in the popular belief, nourished by the Aztec priests, that Quetzalcoatl, a legendary hero who had reigned over the people many years before and had preached a doctrine of peace and love, had been forced to leave the country and cross the great eastern sea but had promised to return and save the nation from its sufferings. Quetzalcoatl was probably the last Toltec ruler, driven out by the invasions of the warlike Aztecs. In the Aztecs' religion he had become a kind of messiah to his people. In recent years Montezuma had been saying, for various reasons, that Quetzalcoatl would soon return: collective hallucinations aroused dreams and visions, in which the Aztecs said that the old sovereign and law-giver would land on the coast and soon come up the valley of Texcoco. It is strange to find fear and not hope in the Aztec songs and poems that mention this, particularly since the legend said that Quetzalcoatl was to bring a time of peace and plenty. The king-god was described as having a fair skin and a beard (whereas all the Indians were clean-shaven), and this made Montezuma think that Cortés might be the reincarnation of Quetzalcoatl. Montezuma was very worried. The Spaniards had reached the edge of the valley and saw before them the city on the lake, with its palaces and towers, its inter-island bridges, some of which seemed to be moveable, on which the people passed; and the lake filled with boats and canoes. This city seemed to them so crowded with life (its population seems to have been between 700,000 and 800,000) that it was like a dream. "Towers, temples, stone and limestone buildings, all built on the water: our soldiers thought they were dreaming. We were seeing then what we had never seen or heard or dreamt of", writes Díaz del Castillo. Then the Mexicans and the Spaniards met. Two civilisations and two worlds came face to face, gazing at each other, questioning each other.

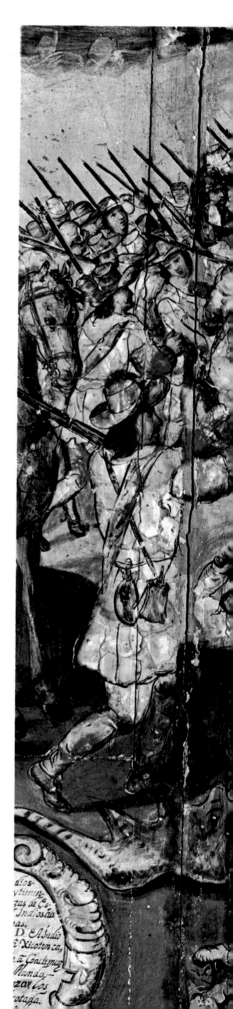

F

G

Above: a remarkable bas-relief on the walls of what is called the "Game of Pelota" at Chichen Itza, in Yucatan. The pre-Conquest Mexicans loved the game and it was played by young people of both sexes. Immediately above: stone image of the plumed serpent, on one of the pilasters of the Temple of the Jaguars at Chichen Itza. This image is often found at the entrance to sacred buildings, not all of which are yet free of the powerful, centuries-old vegetation.

Above and right: details of the
temple of Quetzalcoatl, with
the monstrous heads symbolising
the strength and greatness of the
Toltec hero. Perhaps it was
their last ruler, defeated by
the coming of the Aztecs. It seems
strange that the mild Quetzalcoatl
of the legend, the only beneficient
divinity in the Aztec religion,
the very personification of heaven
and earth and of the union between
day and night, identified with
the planet Venus whose study
was at the basis of astronomy,
protector of the sciences and
the arts, could be represented
as so ugly. Or perhaps this
was merely the self-expression
of a people always threatened by
tragedy.

AN EMBRACE WHICH LOOKED LIKE SACRILEGE

Below: Montezuma moves over to Cortés (detail of one of the panels on the Conquest). In the upper part of the panel we see the natives in their canoes following the royal procession along the canal which surrounded the capital. Left: the meeting between Cortés and the Aztec emperor, in a 19th-century print.

The incident described by Cortés and all the chroniclers of the time, the meeting between the two chiefs and the two peoples, between two armies and two ages, in short between two very disparate worlds, took place on November 8, 1519. The Aztecs had been reigning over this territory, which they had taken from the Toltecs, for nearly two hundred years; the Spaniards had landed that same year. The working people, the whole seething mass that crowded streets, squares and the surrounding water, consisted mostly of Toltecs and other ethnic groups, whereas the Aztecs formed the core of the merchants, soldiers, state officials and dignitaries. Very likely Doña Marina had told Cortés that there was a chance that the non-Aztec ethnic group at the bottom would rebel when the Spaniards arrived, even in the capital, but everything seemed calm. Everyone – Indians and Spaniards – looked at Montezuma, borne on the shoulders of chieftains, in a litter. Everyone wanted to see how he would behave before Cortés-Quetzalcoatl. Centuries of history lay behind the Aztecs: the people of Teotihuacan had built cities and pyramids, the Toltecs had imitated and conquered them, building their masterpiece, the temple of Quetzalcoatl, dedicated to the cult of the plumed serpent, in the same place. When the Aztecs arrived they had proved to be the stronger, and now they found themselves facing a final trial: all those they had conquered were now watching them, waiting to see what would happen in this supremely dangerous contest. Cortés and his men (including the warlike Tlaxcalans) also waited for a gesture from Montezuma, but the emperor studied the stranger: this man, with his proud, direct gaze, dressed in tight, shining armour, surrounded by men at arms, mounted on an unknown monster that cavorted and sent smoke out of its nostrils like a dragon, could he be the mild Quetzalcoatl, the hero of the legends? Montezuma, with 200 men about him, went over to Cortés. In silence he rose from his litter and moved towards the Spaniard. All his men around looked down, since no one was allowed to look him in the face. Cortés went over to embrace him, as a sign of friendship and peace, but two men flung themselves in front of Montezuma to shield him with their bodies and prevent a gesture which to them was sacrilegious.

HISTORICAL MEETING BETWEEN TWO WORLDS

The meeting between Cortés and Montezuma can be compared with the meeting between Caesar and Vercingetorix, between Alexander and the dying Darius, between Marco Polo and Kubla Khan: all meeting between different worlds, when disparate periods of history came together, and gigantic frontiers crumbled. Columbus discovered a new world, Vespucci described its outline, Balboa and Cortés penetrated its living heart. As Marco Polo gave our western civilisation the fascination of China, as Alexander revealed the face of Persia and India, so Cortés unveiled the most important of the great civilisations that had arisen in the American continent, unknown to Europe. The scene was fantastic: pyramids, palaces, cities on the water, dignitaries dressed in precious materials embroidered with gold; men who had discovered the secrets of nature, who used calendars, had calculated the leap year, knew the solstices, mathematical calculations, and writing. The first event in this discovery took place between two remarkable men: a melancholy emperor and a conqueror who, even in the company of his small army, was lonely. Cortés appears to have felt an immediate liking for Montezuma, a tall, well-proportioned, dry and dignified man of about fifty, with a gentle expression, whose manners were extremely charming and who moved gracefully. His first thought was to offer Cortés and his men hospitality that would be worthy of them, and he settled them in a palace with a large central court-yard. When he had rested and felt restored, Cortés sent Doña Marina to the emperor, asking him to meet him at the *teocalli,* the main temple where the Aztecs adored Huitzilopochtli, the god of war. For a long time Montezuma hesitated, then he made up his mind. When Cortés arrived there with nearly all his men, Montezuma was already at the top of the steps, sacrificing human victims. Cortés dismounted from his horse; several Aztecs came forward to help him but he thrust them aside and began climbing the 114 steps. Gradually, as he approached the summit, his heart became frozen with horror: Montezuma was receiving the victims from his priests, and they were then laid on a kind of altar, while he rapidly opened up their breast to take out their hearts. Everything stank of blood, and human limbs were scattered everywhere.

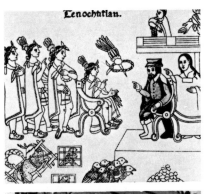

Tenochtitlan.

Above: a page in the Aztec codex, in the Anthropological Museum in Mexico City, showing Montezuma, on the right, with his cloak and regal headdress of feathers, followed by Aztec warriors dragging enemy soldiers. The stylised manner of the drawing is still to be seen in modern Mexican design. Left: three pictures of banquets and receptions held by Cortés and Montezuma. Doña Marina appears in them, as she was interpreter in every conversation between the two men, and Cortés' adviser in his most important decisions. No doubt she had an important influence on the way he behaved towards Montezuma, but we know no details about it. She later disappears abruptly from the story.

39

Right: reconstruction, in the Historical Museum of Mexico City, of Montezuma's regal headdress. It is made of gold and feathers from the quetzal, *a rare bird in the Mexican forests. The original was part of the treasure given by Montezuma to Cortés and sent by him to Charles V. Below: page of the Aztec codex showing a* victim whose heart has been pulled out. This was afterwards wrapped in bandages, like a mummy, to be preserved in honour of Mictlancihuatl, goddess of death. Over the victim is the symbol of the months of the dead. The leitmotiv of the whole Aztec religion was the immolation of victims.*

NO ONE HAD EVER SEEN ANYTHING LIKE IT

Cortés had entered Tenochtitlan without striking a blow, had settled his officers in a palace, and had lodged his men suitably. Then he looked about him and tried to understand the city's social, commercial and religious organization. In one of his letters to the king he praises the beauty of the buildings and particularly notices the beautifully-kept gardens on the terraces and on the plain. He remarks on the wide, straight streets, flanked by canals used by boats bringing farm produce from the surrounding countryside into the city; on the aqueducts that brought fresh water from Chapultepec; on the size and business of the markets. The houses all had flat roofs and there was a causeway on which towers and temples served as fortresses. The Spaniards had never expected such an advanced culture. This proud Spaniard, writing to Charles V, actually said: "The Indians live almost as we do in Spain and in just as orderly a way". Four days after their arrival in the city, on November 12, 1519, Cortés and his most senior officers went with the emperor Montezuma to visit the market and temple of Tlatelolco. They went up to the top of the *teocalli*, that is the shrine of the god, and the emperor, taking Cortés by the hand, told him "to look at this great city and all the other cities situated about the lagoon and the many other villages on dry land. We saw on the lake", Díaz del Castillo continues in his account, "a multitude of ships, some of which leave loaded with goods, and we saw temples and churches, towers and ramparts, houses and terraces, all of a splendid whiteness, and marvellous to behold. And when we had looked at it all we turned to the great market square and to the large crowd buying and selling there: the noise and the sound of voices could be heard more than a league away. Among us there were soldiers who had been in many parts of the world, in Constantinople, in the whole of Italy, in Rome, but they said they had never seen a market so well organised and so orderly, so large and so crowded". Cortés' letters and Lopez de Gomora's diary echo his words: here was a new wonder to be added to the seven wonders of the world known at the time. Montezuma showed Cortés his city, perhaps hoping secretly that he would be fascinated by it and respect it; naturally he had no idea that at that very moment Cortés was planning to take it.

Above: the friar Bartolome de Olmedo, who went with the Spaniards at the time of the Conquest, preaching the Christian faith to Montezuma. Montezuma often reproached the Christians for not having saved their god from death, but to justify the frequent killings demanded by his own religion, he explained that only the lowly were put to death, whereas heroes and brave men, if in disgrace, were exiled. Above: the friendly meeting between Cortés and the emperor Montezuma.

Right: detail of the panels showing the history of the Conquest (American Museum, Madrid): Cortés among his men. Below, top picture: execution of a spy at Xicotenca. Bottom picture: a fight between Spanish and Aztec boats on the water of lake Texcoco, during the conquest of Tenochtitlan.

At the time of the Spanish conquest the Aztecs had reached the height of their power and products from all the surrounding country flowed into the capital: cotton, cocoa, skins and the feathers which the Aztecs used a great deal, precious metals and rare stones. Tenochtitlan was a centre of luxury.

42

THE CAPITAL CITY WITH THE DOUBLE NAME

This page below: from a Mexican codex at the time of the Conquest, a page sent to the court of France to illustrate the position of Tenochtitlan. In the 14th century, the Aztecs came in from the north and reached the shores of Lake Texcoco. Here they received the promised sign from heaven: on an island in the lake, an eagle perched on a cactus, devouring a serpent. There, Mexico-Tenochtitlan was founded. The island was small, the people poor and backward and harried by those who had come before them; they had no stone or wood, but they had a powerful order from the god, immense ambition, and an iron will.

The capital had two names, Mexico-Tenochtitlan, and this double name was explained by a myth and by its geographical position. Mexico meant "in the middle of the lake of the moon"; Tenochtitlan referred to a particular cactus plant. The legend says that an eagle, representing the god Huitzilopochtli, landed on a cactus holding a serpent in its beak. This image, still found today in the arms of the Mexican republic, recalls the mythical tale of the eagle the Aztecs followed in their migration. Where it perched they built their capital city. But in order to do this they had to build a small Venice, for the eagle had landed on an island in lake Texcoco. According to Aztec tradition and by the calculations made according to the country's calendar, this must have taken place in A.D. 1329, the date the Aztecs came to the plateau of Mexico after they had overcome the previous inhabitants, the Toltecs. At the time of the conquest the city of Mexico included the two urban nuclei of Tenochtitlan and Tlatelolco on the islands, and, on the mainland, the coastal village Tepeyacac. The various districts had fascinating names: Toltenco ("the edge of the rushes"), Acatlan ("place of reeds"), Tepetitlan ("beside the hill"), Atlampas ("beside the water") and so on. Altogether the city forms a three kilometre square, covering about 2,500 acres. The work of two centuries had transformed the entire surface into a geometrical net of canals and landing places, centres round two main nuclei: the great temple dedicated to Huitzilpochtli and the main square. Apart from the temple the whole city was divided into four sectors – "the place of flowers", "the district of the god", "the place of mosquitoes" and "the house of the heron". After the Conquest these four districts became the districts of Santa Maria la Redonda, San Pablo, San Juan, and San Sebastian. The sub-divisions were of an administrative kind; each district had its military commander, a temple, a religious school and a house for the young. According to the Spaniards, when they arrived there were about 100,000 houses, containing 7-800,000 inhabitants. Families were large and the ruling classes practiced polygamy, although the first wife took precedence over the others and only her children could inherit. Practical education began at an early age, with children learning to do simple household tasks.

AMAZEMENT AT THE SIGHT OF MEXICAN CIVILIZATION

Cortés' mind was in conflict. He was enchanted with the civilisation he had discovered (as Montezuma had hoped he would be), but at the same time he could not keep to a spectator's role. He and the Aztec emperor were the two main characters in the drama. It was the moment of truth. If a man's valour could be gauged only in times of trouble, as Cortés had learnt in the harsh school of war, then no-one there had yet had his valour tested. Montezuma had so far had an easy reign: the Aztecs had dominated a subject people undisturbed, drowning in blood whatever thoughts of freedom they might have had, and the Spaniards had occupied the country without serious difficulties. But now they were all faced by decisions of immense importance. In the two centuries since they arrived as nomads from the sun-scorched land of California, the Aztecs had founded an enviable civilisation and taken it to its height. Harrassed by the native peoples of the plateau, who were far more civilised than themselves, they chose the valley of Mexico, which was the most easily defended, and overcame the decadent Toltecs. When they abandoned their nomadic way of life and took over the Toltec customs and way of life they imposed their gods and their magical-religious world on those they had conquered. At that time they were divided into twenty groups or clans, called *calpulli*: the land that could be tilled was divided among the group members, on a hereditary basis, and each group had a representative in the *capolec*, at the centre of power. At the head of this was a council of state made up of twelve members of the nobility; and the body made up of representatives of the *calpulli* elected the king. At the beginning the choice was made among members of all the clans, but later on an actual dynasty came into being. Montezuma was the second of that name and the tenth of his house, which had been reigning for 150 years. With the coming of Cortés the dynasty's fate was sealed: the meeting of the two men flung one of the greatest empires and one of the richest civilisations of history into the dust. The Indians of the subjugated tribes did not find a deliverer in the man who conquered the Aztecs; in the end they merely exchanged one imperial power for another. It was as hard to send gold to the king of Spain as it had been to offer tribute to Montezuma.

Above on both pages: details of a series of panels on the Conquest (Museum of America Madrid). Note the scenes showing the first contacts between the conquistadores *and the Aztecs: a friar, Bartolome de Olmedo, preaching to Montezuma; booty being shared out among Cortés' men; traitors being tortured.*

This page above: two typical buildings of Chichen Itza in Yucatan: the castle, and, in front of it, the snail, so called because there was a spiral staircase on the inside. It was an astronomical observatory; the Aztecs knew a great deal about astronomy and mathematics and studied the stars.

Above left: Mexicans trying, unsuccessfully, to pull down a cross set up in front of their idols. Above: symbols of some of the months, in an Aztec calendar. Left: the Pyramid of the Sun and the Way of the Dead in the great sanctuary of Teotihuacan, which contains some of the greatest pre-Conquest buildings of all America. The Mexican temples were in the form of truncated pyramids; staircases and terraces led to the top, where was the great sacrificial stone, two or three holy shrines, and seats for the priests. Nearly all ceremonies culminated in human sacrifices. The victims were often flayed.

RELIGION THE CENTRE OF INDIVIDUAL AND SOCIAL LIFE

Opposite page above: The Square of the Nuns, so called because of the cells looking out on to a central courtyard. Below: the Group of a Thousand Columns, the remains of an immense hall dedicated to religious rites. This page above: a knife used by the priests to extract the victim's heart. The blade is of obsidian, the hilt carved and painted. Below: characterstic sculpture of the divinity at the entrance to the Temple of the Warriors at Chichen Itza. Even women were often sacrificed: as a rule they were beautiful girls who were considered to be "doubles" of female divinities. The priests formed a caste.

In Tenochtitlan, when the Spaniards conquered it, religion was the centre of everyone's life, the determining factor in every activity, from politics to recreation. It was the force that sustained the individual from birth to death; it was therefore the supreme reason for individual action and the basis of the organisation of the state. In the Aztec theocracy, for instance, war was waged more for religious reasons than for anything else, and from the very first day the Spaniards, and particularly Cortés, realised that whatever they wanted from the people they must first get from the priests, rather than from the emperor himself. Montezuma's most trusted councillors were in fact the priests of the temple of Huitzilopochtli, whom he also feared, for in some ways they were more powerful than he was himself. Díaz del Castillo describes their long black robes, their long hair so matted with blood – their own and their victims' – that a comb would not go through it, and the self-inflicted wounds they bore as a sign of penance. The priests could start wars of conquest, because in the new territories they would find slaves to climb the steps of the *teocalli* as victims. More than one priest, in fact, asked Cortés why his god had sent him so far to seek human victims; and, in political discussions, he was also asked if the Aztecs would be enslaved and sacrificed to the Christian god as soon as they were defeated in battle. Religion thus upheld and motivated the Aztec empire, but it also limited its cultural development in a fatal way, by forbidding the introduction of anything new into its rigid structure. Its object was to attract favourable natural forces to human life and to repel those that were unfavourable. Blood, the essence of life, was the price to be paid. Ritual practices, human sacrifices, torture and penance of the faithful tended to make the personifications of these forces, that is the gods, propitious. The Aztecs' original religion was, as far as we know, monotheistic: they adored a single supreme god, Teotl, who was divided into two – one masculine, Ometecuhtli, one feminine, Omecihuatl. Yet a great Aztec pantheon developed later, among which Huitzilopochtli, Tezcatlipoca and Quetzacoatl were especially venerated. Quetzalcoatl, as we have seen, was recognised by the Aztecs and Montezuma himself in the conqueror Cortés.

This page above: a charming
children's story: children not
yet born into the world live on
the fruits of the mannaba in a
kind of heaven. Next picture,
below: prisoners awaiting sentence
of death before the fierce god
of war. Lowest picture: the
prisoner could save his life
if he could defeat four jaguar-men.

THE WAY LIES OPEN FOR A PSYCHOLOGICAL VICTORY

*Opposite page: the god of war,
Huitzilopochtli, his head
adorned with quetzal feathers.
He was the most bloodthirsty of
the Aztec gods; his name means
"Flying-bird"; to him in particular,
human sacrifices were dedicated –
about 20,000 victims a year,
according to a calculation made
by the Spaniards. Cortés tore
down the blood-stained idols.*

After Cortés' rapid conquest, we may wonder what the Aztecs must have thought of their war god, Huitzilopochtli, to whom they had been sacrificing human victims for over 200 years. Did it mean that all these sacrifices and prayers, and the preservation of more than 70,000 skulls of slaves whose breasts had been torn open by the priests to propitiate the god meant nothing? Cortés, the incarnation of Quetzalcoatl, the timid, mild legendary hero of the Toltecs, a weak people already defeated in battle, had returned carrying weapons that thundered, mounted on a monster that ran like the wind. The Aztec warriors knew that there had been valour and cowardice on both sides, that a pitched battle in the open field had not yet been fought; yet the god Huitzilopochtli had allowed Cortés and his *Malinche* to occupy Tenochtitlan, the capital on the water, the invulnerable city. How could Huitzilopochtli, who presided over the tempests, have allowed the Spaniards to go through the mountain-passes, among the craters of the great volcanoes? His favourites, the humming-birds, had given the temple priests no warning, nor had the god himself used his favourite weapon the flaming serpent – that is, the thunderbolt – against the invaders. This is what the ordinary people thought. Montezuma, his nobles and the priests were worried in another way: they knew the Aztec army would not be victorious against the Spaniards. Despite the apparent hopelessness of pitting a small group of Spaniards against great hordes of Indians, Cortés and his men had shown that they could win, not merely because of their guns and horses, but because of their military discipline and more subtle tactics. When Montezuma invited Cortés to a meal and showed him vessels of gold, his masks encrusted with precious stones, his counterfeit hanging gardens in which the flowers had corallas of gold and leaves made of the thinnest quartz, where the gravel on the paths was of rock crystal and the unreal flower-beds trembled in the wind, Cortés doubted that he would ever conquer that empire entirely; and Montezuma, seeing his indecision, thought he might come to an agreement with him. Finally, it seemed as if Cortés had only one way open to him: that of psychological victory. He must put Montezuma in a position of inferiority.

Right: ruins of the monastery of San Domingo at Oaxaca. Below: a little known episode in the Conquest: some Aztecs trying to capture Cortés, who was freed by the intervention of Cristobal de Olea at the head of some faithful Tlaxcalans. Opposite page above: two Aztec warriors carry off a prisoner. Below: an Aztec miniature of the time, showing Montezuma being dressed. Bottom of the page: a portrait of Pedro de Alvarado, whom Cortés left as head of the garrison at Tenochtitlan when he marched against Narvaez. Narvaez was sent by the governor of Cuba to take over command of the Mexican expedition from Cortés.

50

A SPANISH EXPEDITION AGAINST THE REBELLIOUS CORTÉS

As Cortés was ordering Montezuma and his people to pay heavy tributes, in order to lower their morale, news came to him from Veracruz, that is, from the coast, that a Spanish fleet sent by Diego Velazquez, governor of Cuba, was landing men and marching rapidly against him. What Cortés did not know was that Montezuma was in contact with the Spaniards. In fact, the chieftains on the coast had sent messages to the emperor to tell him secretly of the new landings and, secretly too, Montezuma had given orders that the new arrivals should be helped to march against Cortés and given whatever they needed. The emperor also sent word that he was held prisoner, at which Narvaez, leader of the Spanish expedition, replied that Cortés and his men were merely renegades, who in no way represented the king of Spain. Panfilo de Narvaez was an old soldier who, with Velazquez, had taken part in the conquest and colonization of Cuba; he was very loyal to him and as a soldier strictly obeyed the orders he had been given. After sending gold and food supplies to the coast, Montezuma charmingly told Cortés, during a meal, that new ships for him had arrived from Cuba; he did not want to be caught in his deception by Cortés, who was bound to find this out in the end, and had noticed already his increased cheerfulness. Now, Montezuma told him, he could go back to his own country and tell of all he had seen at Tenochtitlan. Cortés took this bad news as best he could, concealed his discomfiture and betrayed nothing. Although extremely worried, he managed to smile at Montezuma and assure him that he would soon decide what to do. As soon as he was back among his own men he held a council of war; the men swore to be loyal to him and were rewarded with gifts of gold. The commander of the garrison at Veracruz sent Cortés a few Spanish prisoners from Narvaez's fleet; Cortés loaded them with rich gifts and sent them back to Narvaez asking him to desist in what he was doing. Narvaez replied by occupying Cempoala. Then, having left Pedro de Alvarado, an enormously tall young captain, in charge of Tenochtitlan, Cortés marched against Narvaez with a smaller force. Alvarado was much loved by Montezuma, who called him "the sun", and this should have favoured Cortés' plans. As it turned out, it did not.

Pedro de Alvarado, a young man of herculean size, had, before he sailed under Cortés, already taken part in the exploration of Yucatan and the Gulf of Mexico. He was very loyal to Cortés and on a number of occasions proved his attachment and courage, but he also caused him a great deal of trouble. It would appear that he had more courage than brains. Before landing on the island of Cozumel Alvarado thought it his duty to sack the villages and remove their inhabitants – indeed, Cortés made him give back what he had taken. In spite of this warning, he repeated his mistake when he was on his own in charge of the capital.

A CRITICAL MOMENT: THE AZTECS IN REVOLT

At this critical moment of his career, Cortés' ability had a chance of showing itself fully. He sent messages to Sandoval, who was in command of the garrison at Veracruz, asking him to join him with his ablest men; he sent spies into Narvaez's camp; and he disguised as Indians some of the Spaniards who spoke a little *Nahuatl,* and made them follow Narvaez's movements step by step and send him messages by friendly Indians who ran day and night in relays. Two hundred and sixty-five men, with 5 horses and 2 cannon, were about to face a warlike army of almost 1,000 armed men, and many cannon and horses. Cortés was to make use of something he had learnt from the Indians, and employ long, copper-tipped lances against the horsemen. He bought the lances from the tribe of the Chinantecs. This time Cortés did not trust his Tlaxcalan allies, and decided to fight the battle on his own. He spoke to his men, and, because he knew them, he did not say that 10, 20 or 40 centuries of history stood watching them from the Aztec or Maya pyramids, but merely that if they won, the gold of Mexico would be divided among the few of them. At night, in driving rain, they set off to make an unexpected attack on Nar-

vaez's camp, which had entrenched itself at Cempoala. Cortés' men took the camp by surprise, which was a great advantage to them: 60 of them, with Sandoval at their head, climbed up to the temples where Narvaez had fortified himself. Narvaez was wounded in the eye with a pike, and in a few minutes it was all over: Cortés' men were masters of Cempoala and of the Spanish camp. The victor spoke to the vanquished, forgave them and promised, if they would follow him, to share the spoils of Mexico with them. Their obvious agreement destroyed any hope Velazquez may have had of overcoming his one-time subordinate's rebellion. But at the very moment in which 2,000 Mexicans – when all was over – arrived to help him, news reached Cortés that Tenochtitlan was in revolt, Alvarado had been overthrown and the Spaniards massacred. Having triumphed cunningly and cleverly over Narvaez, Cortés now saw everything ruined by Alvarado's stupid abuse of power and lack of diplomacy. Fate once again seemed against him: another man might have lost heart, but not Cortés. From his grave danger he drew new strength, and made it the culminating incident of his conquest.

Left: a god of death seizes a prisoner by the hair. This is the old theme of violence, repeated cruelly throughout the Aztec religion. The thousands of victims stretched out on the altars of the cruel priest had no effect, of course: the prophetic legend of Quetzalcoatl's return was now to be fulfilled. Below: the small god Xolotl climbs on to the plant of life. At the sides are two priests and at the bottom the head of Tlaloc, god of rain, who sucks the spring water with his tongue to change it into a precious life-giving fluid. Tlaloc welcomed into heaven those who had died violently, or from certain sacred diseases.

HIS ENEMIES DEFEATED, CORTÉS FACES THE MEXICANS

When he had defeated Narvaez's army and taken his officers prisoner, Cortés sent Francesco da Lugo to the sea with orders to bring back all the ships' captains and equipment from the 18 ships which Diego Velazquez had sent against him from Cuba. In this way he made certain that no-one would flee to the Antilles to give the news of his victory. He feared that Velazquez would be so angry if he heard of it that he would prepare another, more powerful army. Then, when he had made sure of the coast and occupied every possible landing place with loyal troops, he turned his attention to Tenochtitlan, where conditions were very serious. Pedro de Alvarado had not been up to the task Cortés had given him. He was young and hot-headed, and not really experienced enough to bear such a responsibility. As a result he put the lives of all his company in jeopardy. When he left, Cortés tried to take all possible precautions and sent Montezuma into the fortified palace which he had made his own headquarters. Cortés' 19th century detractors say that Montezuma was kept there in chains, but there is nothing to make us believe it. Bernal Díaz del Castillo says clearly that when Cortés returned to Mexico city: "Montezuma went up to him and tried to embrace and welcome him, but Cortés refused even to see him, and poor Montezuma went back to his room, sad and thoughtful". It was Pedro de Alvarado, in fact, who put about the legend of Montezuma's imprisonment and of his ill-treatment, and even said that while Cortés was at the coast fighting Narvaez, Montezuma had given secret orders to his men to fling down all the Christian images set up by Cortés on the Aztec pyramids and temples. But Alvarado may have been resentful after defeat. If Montezuma had really been a prisoner and watched by his guards in the fortress – which the Spaniards grandly called the Palace – then it is hard to see how he could have been in secret contact with some of his followers, very few of whom, in any case, would have been ready to risk the Spanish commander's anger by knocking down crosses and statues of the Madonna at night. Díaz del Castillo says that the chieftains had made a spell to cast a Christian image down from the great pyramid, but that Montezuma himself had made it known that he wanted it left where it was.

Left-hand page: 19th-century picture showing Cortés giving orders for chains to be put round the ankles of the astonished Montezuma. Beside the sovereign is Doña Marina, who looks pleased, while his followers seem astounded by such an unfriendly act. There is no historical basis for this incident however. This page above: 17th-century engraving showing Alvarado and his men attacking the Mexicans to seize their gold; and an Aztec miniature showing the Mexican warriors at the attack on the palace where Montezuma was living during Cortés' absence. Above: another 19th-century picture: Cortés says goodbye to Montezuma before leaving for the coast to meet Narvaez. Note the contrast between this picture and that on the previous page, although they are contemporary. From what Cortés wrote it appears that he actually entrusted the Spaniards to the emperor.

MONTEZUMA'S MYSTERIOUS DEATH

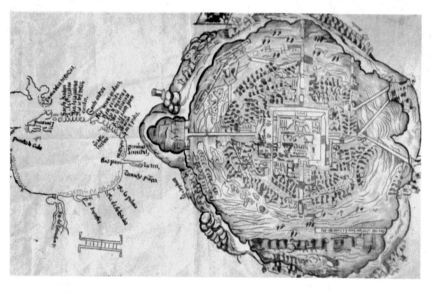

A few days after Cortés had left Tenochtitlan, the feast in honour of Huitzilopochtli, god of war, must have taken place in the temple quite near the district where the Spaniards were quartered and where the palace stood in which Montezuma was half-imprisoned. Alvarado gave permission for the temple to be used, but suddenly attacked those officiating, with the excuse that he had heard of a plan to attack the Spanish garrison. A furious fight broke out. At the end of it over 600 Aztecs and 7 Spanish soldiers lay dead in the temple courtyard. But the revolt spread to the whole city: a rumour went about that the Spaniards were killing the priests, and a raging mob attacked the soldiers, who had to shut themselves up in their own quarters. Thus Cortés found them when he arrived back after a forced march from the coast. At first he could get no further than Texcoco, one of the outlying districts of the city, because armed Aztec warriors hurled themselves on him from all sides and the city thronged with shrieking crowds, demanding vengeance. The Spaniards attacked the city many times, until they made a fortified camp around Montezuma's palace, which was immediately besieged. Cortés forced Montezuma to speak to his people, but his appearance was greeted with arrows and stones. A stone struck his head and he fell back. He was taken to his apartment, but refused all help, and a little later, Díaz del Castillo wrote, "to our great surprise, those who were with him came to tell us that Montezuma was dead". His death was mysterious, and its mystery will never be solved. It ended the period of co-existence between the Spaniards and the Mexicans, who doubtless thought he had been murdered: open war now broke out.

This page above: a feast celebrated beside one of the pyramids of Tenochtitlan. This was the feast of flowers, during which young girls were sacrificed. In the foreground are the terrible Jaguar warriors. There was a similar feast in honour of the god of war, during which the Aztec revolt broke out. While his people were in revolt, Montezuma was practically imprisoned in the Palace. Above right: a 17th-century print showing dancers performing in honour of Montezuma. Immediately above: a fine map of Tenochtitlan, attributed to Cortés himself. Opposite page: the culminating incident of the Aztec revolt: Montezuma is forced to speak to his people. These were the last moments of his life. A little later, after being hit by a stone which was flung at him, he allowed himself to die, putting up no opposition to the fate that had picked him as its tragic victim, and believing that there was a higher will against which it was useless to fight.

THE "NOCHE TRISTE": CORTÉS FIGHTS HIS WAY THROUGH

Cortés decided to retire from Tenochtitlan, and fought his way out in a long, cruel desperate battle. Nearly all the men he had captured from Narvaez fell into the Aztecs' hands and were sacrificed to the god of war and dragged screaming to the altars, to have their hearts cut out of their breasts. As they retired, the Spaniards burnt every house, destroyed the temples, flung the idols into the canals, and killed without a pause. Every man of Cortés' army was wounded, and Cortés cursed Alvarado and his hot-bloodedness which had destroyed what he had built up with so much patience and diplomacy. Montezuma's death must have saddened him, but now, whatever happened, he had to get out of the city which was burning beneath his feet. At one point the Indians attempted to pen them in and burn them alive. The night of his retreat was the famous *noche triste,* the sad night, which the chroniclers and historians have written so much about. Sword in hand, Cortés and his officers fought every yard of the way, while the soldiers seized whatever gold, jewels and other treasures they could lay hands on. Many were so weighed down with it that they could not cross the canals and were drowned or caught by Aztec warriors and finished off with truncheon blows. A group of soldiers retreated, surrounding Doña Marina. They fought in the blood that ran along the alleyways. Marina managed to escape on horseback while Cortés, taking advantage of a moment's break, tried to rally the surviving Spaniards. The Tlaxcalans remained faithful until death: at the last canal they formed a wall and, while the Spaniards crossed, allowed themselves to be massacred. For 6 days the Aztecs trailed the Spaniards closely, their numbers constantly increasing, and the Spaniards fought without rest. Some of them died of exhaustion and hunger. On the seventh day a few hundred men clung, weary and exhausted, to the rocks above the valley of Otumba. In a week of fighting they had covered 23 miles. Suddenly, after a brief rest, Cortés rose and spoke to his men. It seems incredible, but he gave a single order, a mad, absurd order that sounded like an insult to that band of hungry, wounded men: "Attack"! And yet the bleeding, exhausted band, wounded, bruised, limping and famished, rose in a body, and, like an army of ghosts, counter-attacked.

The death of Montezuma only served to infuriate the Mexicans, and Cortés was obliged to take flight. This happened on the night of June 30, 1520 – the famous noche triste. *Two pictures illustrate this, at the top a panel of the conquest, across two pages, and immediately above in an Aztec miniature.*

*Left and above: two other
details from the* noche triste.
*An enemy city had to be crossed
without arousing suspicion.
The Spaniards returned under cover
of a furious storm, but not
before they had first loaded
themselves up with gold. When
the storm suddenly stopped, and*
*the Mexicans had been aroused by
a screaming woman, they were
caught while crossing the lake
on an improvised bridge. Many
fell under the tragic weight
they were carrying. Above right:
the church of the Zocalo in
Mexico City, built on the spot
where the Great Pyramid stood.*

59

Right, and in the large 19th-century painting below: two incidents in the mortal battle Cortés fought with the Aztec commander and finally won. At that moment Cortés summed up all his men's desperate will to conquer. These men, who had left a life of poverty at home, called themselves hidalgos as soon as they boarded the ship that was to take them to the New World, rebelled against the constituted authority as soon as they arrived there, and now had to defend their nobility, although it was merely invented. They could never return to Spain unless they were rich and victorious.

THE LAST DECISIVE BATTLE, AT OTUMBA

It was June 7, 1520. In the valley of Otumba, surrounded by thousands of Aztec warriors mad for blood, Cortés fought what he thought was his last battle, the one that would sum up his whole life, the greatest of his many adventures. At one point, in the sea of dead and wounded, he saw an Aztec chieftain fighting, dressed in coloured feathers and a gaudy cloak. With Sandoval, Alvarado and two or three others around him, Cortés fought his way over to this enemy leader, met him in a single combat and killed him. When the man in the plumed cap fell, the Aztecs fled. At night, the Spaniards went across the battlefield at Otumba, almost dropping with wounds and weariness: they were walking over a sea of dead Aztecs. Tlaxcala, the faithful city, was chosen by the Spaniards for rest and re-organization. They were now a tiny army, but firmly determined to conquer the capital on the water. A nephew of Montezuma, Cuauhtemoc, whom the Spanish chroniclers called Guatimozimo, was now reigning and collecting troops from every part of his empire, determined to pursue the Spaniards into the sea. But now, under Cortés' orders, these Spaniards were actually doing military exercises and practising guerrilla warfare in the mountains round Tlaxcala, punishing the rebel tribes. Cortés was waiting for reinforcements from all the Spanish territories, including even Cuba, and was already making plans for a reconquest. Meanwhile he freed those men who had come with Narvaez and now wanted to return to Cuba to tell of their adventures. His subtle diplomacy was at work again; at the same time he showed his extreme efficiency by ordering a certain Martin Lopez and other carpenters to make a fleet of canoes: he must capture the capital on the lake.

Above left: old print showing the fierce battle in the valley of Otumba. Above right: a monument in memory of the fallen Aztecs, put up by the modern Mexicans. The slaughter was appalling. To conquer the capital Cortés had a handful of weary, wounded but unconquered men.

Immediately above: family tree of the emperor Montezuma: the last person on the right is his nephew Cuauhtemoc who succeeded him, led the revolt against the Spaniards and died in mysterious circumstances. (Mexican painting on a leaf of American aloe).

CORTÉS ADVANCES ON THE CAPITAL WITH NEW TROOPS

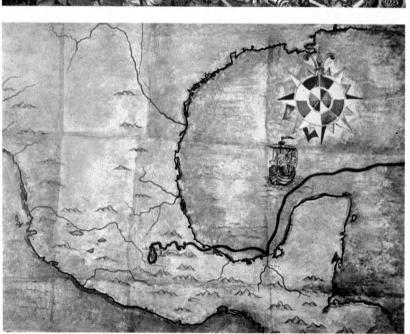

Reinforced by men and arms that had come to him from the Canary Isles, from Jamaica, from Spain, and even from Cuba – where Velazquez thought his lieutenant Narvaez was in charge of the situation – Cortés' army, assisted by fresh troops from Tlaxcala, soon came within sight of Tenochtitlan. For two days the Spaniards waited around the lake while Cortés planned his attack. The towns nearby were beginning to send him messages of peace and submission. Cortés himself sent Indian emissaries to Cuauhtemoc, offering him peace if he would allow the Spaniards to enter the city, but the emperor ignored this request. Cortés then loaded up the boats built by Martin Lopez and dug a canal to allow them to reach the lake. At the same time he discovered a counterplot against himself organised by some of Narvaez's ex-soldiers and led by Antonio de Villafana, who was executed. On April 28, 1521, the feast of Pentecost, the Spanish fleet sailed and the fight with the Aztecs began. Cortés had replenished his armoury by getting the friendly towns in the region to make him 50,000 arrowheads to a Spanish pattern. He also ordered special training sessions for the horsemen. For several days the fighting was feeble. It was only on May 26 that the main body of the troops, led by Alvarado and Olid, attacked the aqueducts that took fresh water into the city. On May 21 Cortés himself led his fleet against the enemy fortress: he landed before anyone else, climbed the ramparts and seized the Aztec fortress that had been set up as the city's main defence. At the same time about 1,500 enemy ships closed in behind him. A furious battle followed, while a bold move by Sandoval on the opposite side completely surrounded the city. The Spaniards stayed on the mainland, firing on the Aztec canoes, while Cortés and his men penned about 300,000 warriors inside Tenochtitlan. For about three weeks hand to hand fighting went on: they fought from house to house, flinging their wounded enemies into the canals. The Spaniards fought with incredible ferocity to avoid being taken prisoner. On August 12 a Spanish ship captured a canoe: it was carrying the emperor Cuauhtemoc. When he was brought before his conqueror the "fallen eagle" said: "I have come only because, as a prisoner, I am forced to: take the sword you have by your side and kill me."

Cortés at last receives the reinforcements he has been awaiting and can attack the capital. Left-hand page, from top to bottom: an allegory of the conquest; Cortés' route to reoccupy Tenochtitlan (on a 16th-century map); the fleet of Cuauhtemoc trying to break out. The emperor was captured in a canoe. This page, above: Cortés' triumphant entry into the captured capital; left: detail of the scene in Tenochtitlan as seen by Aztec artists in a Tlaxcalan codex.

The Spaniards fought very fiercely: they knew that if they were captured they would be sacrificed alive on the pyramids in the city. Cortés himself climbed the walls of the Aztec fortress and left a garrison.

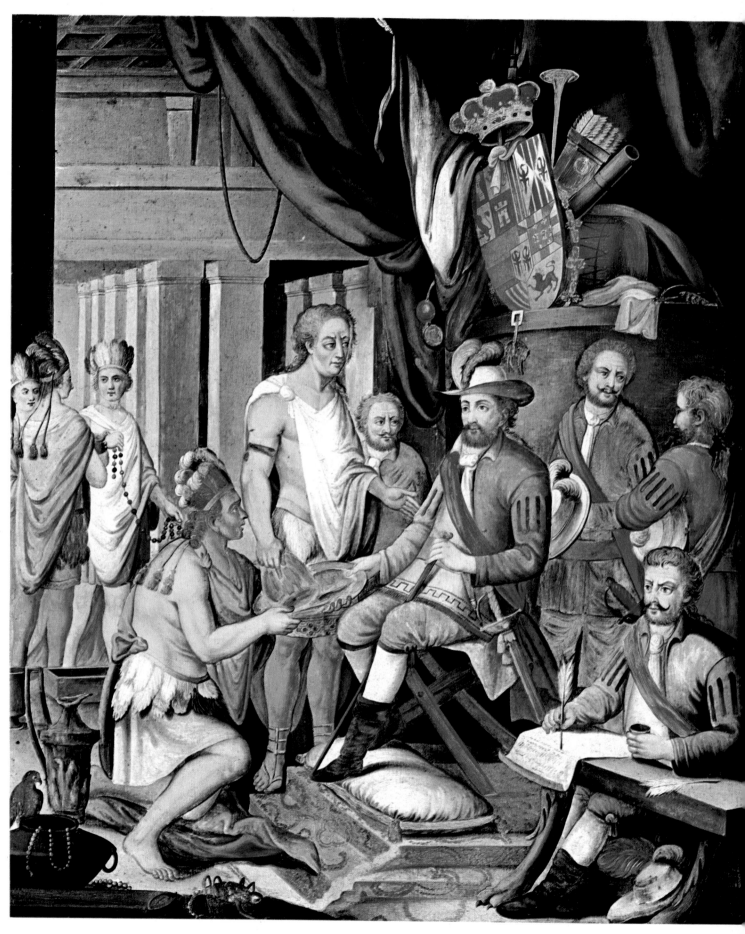

MYSTERIOUS DEATH OF THE LAST AZTEC EMPEROR

Opposite page: Cortés on the throne of the Aztec emperors receives the leaders of the tribes. This page: three different interpretations of the capture of Cuauhtemoc, last emperor of Mexico: above, left: from the Lienzo de Tlaxcala: further left: from an 18th-century picture, and below in a print.

The Spanish conqueror, with Doña Marina at his side, received the captured emperor in an atmosphere of unaccustomed silence. For months the air had been filled with the war-cries of the Indians and the sound of their drums; now all was still. Cortés rose and welcomed him cordially, and the prisoner said he had done all he could to defend himself and his people. The siege had lasted 85 days. With the complete destruction of its capital, the Aztec empire had crumbled. At this point the reports of the chroniclers who were eye-witnesses end, and the death of Cuauhtemoc remains as mysterious as that of Montezuma. The black legend – that is, the version given by Cortés' detractors – says that Cortés tortured the emperor to make him reveal where the royal treasure was hidden. Another tradition says that he took the emperor with him on an expedition to Honduras. Whatever really happened, Cuauhtemoc was finally executed. Left alone in the now tragic country, Cortés at last saw his efforts recognised. On October 15, 1522, a royal order arrived, nominating him governor and captain-general of New Spain and giving him full powers to explore the country extensively. He then began sending some of his captains on explorations: Pedro de Alvarado was sent to Guatemala, Cristobal de Olid to Honduras, others left for Nicaragua and Panama, and others discovered California. Nuno de Guzman conquered and opened up land between the western Sierra Madre and the Pacific. Cortés himself took part in the discovery of the Pacific coasts of New Spain. In the same months troops of bureaucrats – notaries, clerks, administrators and officials – arrived from Spain, together with ever increasing numbers of Franciscan friars.

In a final effort to persuade the nearby peoples to fight with him against Cortés, the Aztec emperor played on the "blood bond" between them. He sent out ambassadors to say that the white man was the sole enemy and that they must form a holy alliance around Tenochtitlan. He proposed changing the Aztec empire into a confederation of equals. This idea, which might have saved the empire, came too late. The tribes, which had submitted for so long, remembered the Aztec yoke with bitterness and horror, the hostages they had had to give to be sacrificed in honour of cruel gods their masters worshipped, the heavy tributes they had had to pay, and the pride of their rulers.

THE COMMAND PASSES TO THE BUREAUCRATS FROM SPAIN

Very soon Cortés let himself be dominated by the bureaucrats, partly because he was involved in his explorations. The band of *conquistadores* split up, as they were sent to subdue the allies and tributary provinces of Mexico. Soon, too, the temptations to use the Indians as slaves proved too great and every Spaniard in New Spain in some way abused the conquered people. To Cortés' credit it must be stressed that he and a few other great and enlightened Spaniards, like Bishop Zumarraga and Vasco de Quiroga, did what they would to defend the rights of the Indians; and it was not his fault that, although he was governor, he was able to do little. The situation grew even worse when, in 1534, Charles V nominated Antonio de Mendoza Viceroy of New Spain, with absolute authority. Recent historians have pointed out that Cortés quarrelled endlessly with Mendoza, and with the royal auditors and other bureaucrats, not over silly matters of etiquette but because he was trying to defend the rights of the Aztecs, whereas all they cared about was sending treasure to Veracruz to load up the king's ships. At last they built a magnifi-

cent palace at Cuernavaca and invited him to retire there; but for a little longer he struggled on, trying to help the country he had conquered. Naturally enough, men like Cortés are an embarrassment once their task is over: the same thing had been found with Columbus. Charles V gave him the title of Marquis of the Valley of Oaxaca, and allowed him to keep great riches for himself, to own a huge estate and as many slaves as he wished. But he had to submit to the humiliation of seeing the magistrates sent from Spain set about organising the country according to orders and standards that had nothing to do with him, and, in the process, ignoring and excluding him. Even Díaz del Castillo says: "After he had conquered New Spain he had no luck in anything". Cortés, a solitary, often misunderstood hero throughout the campaign, was to end his life alone, if not forgotten. At the end of his life his stature did not, perhaps, increase like that of other unfortunate leaders, yet his inability to make himself heard in the world which he himself created from the beginning gives him, for us, a certain tragic importance.

Far left, opposite page: portrait of Antonio Mendoza, who in 1534 was sent as Viceroy of New Spain, that is, of the country conquered by Cortés, to whom it was a great blow, for it meant he was superseded by officials sent by the mother country. Cortés, shown on the same page in an Aztec portrait, had interminable quarrels with Mendoza. Left, top of both pages: the splendid house Cortés had built at Cuernavaca. Below: an allegory of a subjected Mexico, in which the Aztecs take up their work in the fields and mines again, while the Spaniards organise every activity and pitilessly brand their slaves.

Below: in one of the panels in the Museum of America in Madrid, Father Bartolome de Olmeda blesses ships and sailors soon to set off to explore new parts of central America. This monk had followed Cortés' expedition from the beginning. Later Charles V himself sent Father Juan Zumarraga, whose integrity he knew well, as first bishop of his new territories, a man who did honour to the position he had been entrusted with, who showed fairness and defended the Indians, trying to integrate them in a new Christian community that was at once Spanish and Mexican. In the end the Church could not protect them however.

While the Spaniards were enlarging the frontiers of their conquered territory, Cortés settled Doña Marina by marrying her to Juan Jaramillo, one of his officers. Afterwards, we hear no more of her. Hernan Cortés' brilliant career was now nearing its end. Montezuma and Cuauhtemoc had their revenge, paradoxically, through the Spanish bureaucrats and through Francisco de los Cobos, Charles V's secretary, whom Cortés had rashly antagonised. Everything he did, every order he gave, was checked and revised with the minutest care. All his accounts were examined by the royal clerks. The Spanish crown had spent nothing on the conquest of New Spain, yet its bureaucrats knew that the surest way to discredit a too-popular hero was to accuse him of not having handed over the percentage he owed the crown. Columbus had already been shamefully accused of this, and so had Gonzalo Fernandez de Cordoba, who had conquered southern Italy. None of the captains who had faithfully stood by Cortés in all the danger and hardship he had known achieved the riches or even the peaceful independent life for which they had hoped. Even the distribution, publication and translation of the letters Cortés had written to the king was forbidden. Cortés then went back to Spain, for what he thought would be a short visit, to reinstate himself; but the journey was unsuccessful and he returned to Mexico to continue his explorations. In 1530, he undertook a difficult and courageous expedition to lower California; then, still surrounded by the envious and still accused of corruption, he set off again for Spain. There he tried to be received by Charles V, but in vain. One day, in Valladolid, he suffered the final humiliation of having to approach the emperor in the street to hand him a document. Charles V pushed away the piece of paper and asked one of those in his train. "Who is this man?" The old adventurer raised himself to his fullest height and answered proudly: "I am the man who gave Your Majesty more kingdoms than you inherited cities from your ancestors!" However, this proud answer had no effect at all. The king was tired and busy himself; he no longer felt any enthusiasm for government and thought more of retiring to the studies he loved. Cortés and his men were treated as untrustworthy adventurers. For Cortés, this meant the end.

Left: the first church built by the Spaniards in Yucatan, near the present-day Merida. Below that: the frontispiece of the collection of letters which Cortés sent to the emperor Charles V, now at Brown University. The sovereign is surrounded by his court as he receives the petitions of Cortés. Bottom left: the university built by the Spaniards at Morellin, 50 years after the Conquest. Immediately below: 18th-century print showing an Aztec cemetery; below that: one of the first codices which Fra Bernardino da Sahagun got the Mexicans to make. Top: a monk pours holy water over one of the Aztec divinities.

Right: a famous portrait of Cortés by an unknown painter, in the Historical Museum of Mexico City. Below: two engravings showing typical games played by the young Aztecs. The conquered population kept its own traditions and at the start was reluctant to take over the Spanish way of life.

HE DIES IN SPAIN WITHOUT SEEING MEXICO AGAIN

Below, top picture: an ingenious representation of the Creed made by Aztec converts. Bottom picture: one of the oldest monasteries built by Spanish missionaries in the state of Oaxaca. At the beginning there were not many conversions and the Aztecs professed their ancient faith in secret, but the lack of a priestly caste and the total prohibition of their cruel rites gradually made them forget the religion of their fathers. Later, the humblest Mexicans took up the new faith enthusiastically and produced spectacular celebrations in honour of the Virgin Mary and the other saints. But traces of the past linger.

Cortés wantéd to die in Mexico, but could not get leave to set sail. While far away, in New Spain, Mexico City was being built according to his original plans, and he was trustfully waiting to embark, Cortés died on December 2, 1547, at the age of 62, at Castilleja de la Cuesta, near Seville. He had asked his family to have his remains taken to Mexico, but it was only several decades later, in 1629, that his body found peace where Montezuma had met his mysterious death. In the whole history of the American continent, there is nothing to compare with Cortés' achievements. His intelligence, his sensibility, his clearsightedness and the great sympathy he felt for his Mexican adversaries have nothing in common with the deliberate ferocity of Pizarro in Peru. The killings attributed to him by the black legend – the massacre at Cholula and the rather ambiguous deaths of Montezuma and Cuauhtemoc – do not cancel out the personal valour and military virtues that were considered the highest attributes in a man of the Renaissance. Faced with a culture which was as firmly based and coherent as his own, and yet contravened all its most sacred laws, Cortés seems to have gone a long way towards understanding the Aztecs. The fact that he turned the native tribes against one another was obviously part of the game of power and conquest. We do not know how much influence on his decision his lieutenant's behaviour had, whereas we do know how much he regretted what Alvarado did in provoking the *noche triste,* and it is well known that he showed generosity even to his staunchest enemies, like Narvaez. Díaz del Castillo considered him a hero in the highest sense of the word, comparable only with Caesar and Alexander, although he gave his officers the credit they deserved as well; while Lopez de Gomara and other minor chroniclers made him a symbol for later generations of Spaniards. Historically, Cortés was the first adventurer from our western civilisation to make contact with a great political and social organization created by "coloured people": he then felt that he had a mysterious superiority which, though he could not define it exactly himself, was powerful and decisive. He was upheld and given confidence by this and made of it a weapon of power and glory for himself and for Spain.

HIS NAME IS INDISSOLUBLY LINKED WITH MEXICO

A visitor today, passing through the streets of Mexico City, Veracruz, Tlaxcala or Cholula, will find no statues of Cortés. National pride, and the resurgence of literary, artistic and folklore traditions, which have tended to reconsider the ancient Mexican civilisation, have made the people make Aztecs like Cuauhtemoc heroes – though not the rash and unlucky Montezuma – and leave Cortés' work to students of history. Yet the streets of those cities will always reflect what Cortés did – in the fortifications which still exist, in the palaces that have escaped so many revolutions, in the tranquil convents, in the embankments that have filled up the canals, in the steady, slightly surprised looking faces of the people, who have still kept some of the customs that Cortés and his soldiers found in the highlands, when they arrived in search of gold and glory. The time of great conquests is over, and so is the age of colonialism; Cortés' epic now remains the almost desperate adventure of a Renaissance gentleman, lonely through his contemporaries' lack of understanding and interest, uncertain over decisions that might offend the human dignity of others like himself, yet confident in following his own destiny. In present day Mexican festivals, the figure of Cortés never appears; yet his spirit is always present, for every year anniversaries are celebrated recalling the final events of the Aztec empire, events that still show Hernan Cortés as a triumphant "gentleman adventurer", whatever his detractors may have accused him of, and however excessively his admirers may have praised him. Whenever the archaeologist's spade digs up a stone, a weapon, or skeleton belonging to the proud civilisation of the Aztecs, inevitably one must remember the man who, though with blood and fire, revealed that great nation to the entire world. The figure of Hernan Cortés is linked forever, and indissolubly, with Mexico, as he himself would have wished: his soldiers, his horses, the battles he fought, the *noche triste,* the traitors, the spies, the patriots, all made present-day Mexico, the Latin-American country into which Spain poured her whole self, and in which she is still to be clearly seen. Perhaps the Spanish language, heard throughout the country, is the most vital memorial Cortés could have.

This page above: the majestic palace, several times restored, built on the site where Montezuma's royal palace stood. Left: Cortés in his uniform of captain-general. Opposite page: in the centre, two examples of 16th-century Spanish architecture in Mexico. Above: the church and convent of Patzcuaro; below: the ancient palace of the royal officials. Far left: the so-called Square of the Three Civilisations. In the foreground are the remains of an Aztec temple, in the middle a church built by the Spanish conquerors, and in the distance the building of modern Mexico City, which now no longer recalls even the site of the ancient Mexico-Tenochtitlan, which rose out of the water, queen of all the cities built in central America before the Conquest. After the sufferings caused by the old colonialists, it is probably natural enough that their memory is not revered. Yet Mexico does owe a debt to them, and not least to the man who led the first venture, whose courageous example could turn defeat into victory, as he showed in the battle of Otumba, and incompetent men like Pedro de Alvarado into proud and loyal officers.

We close this story of Cortés' feats with a beautiful picture of the Castle of Chichen Itza. Cortés gave Spain a country that was both enormous and enormously rich, and took from one of the greatest pre-Conquest civilisations the strength that upheld it. The Aztecs had conquered Mexico bloodily, when they seized it from the peaceful Toltecs, and then themselves surrendered in blood. To them, Cortés really seemed a man sent by the gods, for the emperor Montezuma saw in him the incarnation of the Toltec hero Quetzalcoatl, pursued from his own dominions centuries earlier. This was one of the basic reasons for the success of Cortés and his handful of desperate men. Yet Montezuma's fears and hesitations would have meant nothing if, on the battlefield of Otumba, a single man had not made a small band of famished, wounded, harried men into a handful of heroes and recaptured an empire.

We have enough information to make up a physical portrait of Hernan Cortés ("he was of medium stature, not very hairy, witty and lively, and a lover of women . . .", says Jose Suarez de Peralta), but we know very little of what passed through his mind during the great adventure that has brought his name down to us. We know very little about his religion; about his caution in taking definite decisions; about the kind of affection that linked him to other human beings, both men and women; about the sincerity of some of his actions. On many occasions we see him sad, in many cases hesitant, reluctant to threaten the rights of others yet pitiless in applying the rules of war. Did he love Doña Marina? We do not know. Was he really fascinated by Montezuma? We can only suppose he was from some of his attitudes, but others deny it. Did he have faith in himself? One thing is certain: he never hesitated in his wish to conquer Mexico, and he finally had Mexico at his feet. The strength of the enemy, the intrigue of his compatriots, the obstacles of nature: none of these could stop him. Cortés, like Columbus, exists only in the light of what he did. He wanted Mexico and this was the only reality that counted for him. All the rest (and all other people) were dimmed in his eyes.

1485 – Born at Medellin, Estremadura, to Martin Cortés de Monroy and Dona Cataline Pizarro Altamirano.
1492 – January 2: Ferdinand of Aragon and Isabella of Castile enter Granada, the last Arab stronghold in Spain.
August 3: Columbus set sail from Palos.
October 12: Columbus sights the American continent.
1499 – Cortés is a law student at Salamanca and stays there two years.
1504 – He leaves Spain for Santa Domingo, the island which Columbus had called Hispaniola.
1511 – He is under the orders of Diego Velazquez in the conquest of Cuba.
1511–2 – Jeronimo de Aguilar and Gonzalo Guerrero, shipwrecked on an expedition to Darien, reach Yucatan and hear of a great empire in the highlands.
1513 – September 29: Vasco Nunez de Balboa first catches sight of the Pacific ocean.
1518 – Expedition of Juan de Gribjalba to the coast of Mexico. November: Cortés leaves Santiago de Cuba, sent by Velazquez to explore Mexico ("the mysterious country of the west").
1519 – March 23: the expedition reaches the river Tabasco. Doña Marina is offered to Cortés by the native chiefs.
July: Foundation of Veracruz. Cortés gets himself nominated captain-general, thus repudiating any possibility of submitting to Velazquez. Here he receives the messengers of Montezuma II; he disarms and sinks his own ships to discourage any attempt his troops might have to desert, and on August 16 starts his march towards the interior of the country with 508 foot soldiers, 16 horse-

men, and 6 pieces of artillery. September: first skirmishes with the men of Tlaxcala. September 18: enters Tlaxcala. October 12: continues his advance towards Mexico – Tenochtitlan, capital of the Aztec empire. October 16: massacre at Cholula. November 1 the expedition sets out again. November 8: Cortés is welcomed by Montezuma at Tenochtitlan. November 14: Cortés makes Montezuma move to the palace.
1520 – Velazquez sends fleet to Juan de Ulua, under the command of Panfilo de Narvaez. May 29: Cortés defeats him at Cempoala, and, reinforced by Narvaez's contingent of men, who have submitted to him, hastens to Tenochtitlan, where Pedro de Alvarado's behaviour has provoked the Mexicans to rise against him. June 24: Cortés manages to re-enter Tenochtitlan. June 27: Montezuma is forced to try to calm his people, but is greeted with a shower of stones. He is seriously wounded and dies under mysterious circumstances. June 28: after an Aztec attack the Spaniards leave the city at night. June 30–July 1: the *noche triste*: rout of the Spanish army. Cortés and his officers fight their way out. July 7: Spanish counter-attack in the valley of Otumba; the Mexicans put to flight. September 7: Cuauhtemoc becomes emperor of the Aztecs and hastens to defend the capital, now attacked by Cortés, who has re-formed his army at Tlaxcala.
1521 – May 26: The Spaniards attack Tenochtitlan and cut the aqueduct. June 9: Cortés and his men fight their way to the Great Pyramid. June 30: the Spaniards' first great assault on the capital fails. July 20: in the second they seize some houses. August 12:

Cuauhtemoc captured in a canoe. The capital surrenders.
1522 – October 15: Charles V recognises Cortés' conquest and names him captain-general and governor.
1524 – Exploration of Honduras by Cortés.
1525 – February: mysterious death, possibly by execution, of the last Aztec emperor. In the same year Cortés falls into disfavour with the crown.
Strange metal, possibly platinum, found in Mexico.
1526 – July: arrival in Mexico of a commissary named by the king, to inquire into accusations against Cortés.
Francisco de Pizarro reaches Peru.
1528 – March 17: Cortés embarks for Spain, hoping to clear his name.
1529 – He is created Marquis of the Valley of Oaxaca and confirmed in his position as captain-general with the task of continuing his discoveries.
1530 – July: Cortés returns to Mexico.
1532 – Francisco de Pizarro destroys the empire of the Incas.
1534 – Madrid sends Antonio de Mendoza as Spain's first viceroy in Mexico.
1535 – Pizarro founds Lima.
1540 – Cortés, ignored in the country he conquered, returns to Spain to press his rights.
1541 – He takes a courageous part in the expedition against the Algerians.
1542 – Las Casas' account of the Conquest published.
1547 – December 2: Cortés dies, aged 62, at Castilleja de la Cuesta, near Seville, embittered by his failure to be given proper recognition, and after trying in vain to get permission to return to Mexico.

PORTRAITS OF GREATNESS

General Editor
ENZO ORLANDI

Text by
ROBERTO BOSI

Translator
ISABEL QUIGLEY

Published 1969 by
The Hamlyn Publishing Group Ltd
Hamlyn House, The Centre,
Feltham, Middlesex
© 1968 Arnoldo Mondadori Editore
Translation © 1969 by
The Hamlyn Publishing Group Ltd
Printed in Italy by
Arnoldo Mondadori, Verona